SPIRIT REALM
– the Reality

Extraordinary real life experiences

Plus keys to spiritual growth and the exercising of supernatural powers

Adrian Denyer

First published 2018 by Adrian Denyer, Tauranga, New Zealand.

Further copies of this book in either Kindle or Print format can be obtained from:

www.amazon.com

ISBN   978-0-473-42970-6 Print
              978-0-473-42971-3 Kindle

Any suggestions or comments, contact the author at denyeradrian27@gmail.com

Contents

Preface

My name is Adrian and I'm about to take you on a journey that I hope will open your eyes and your mind.

This is an honest and truthful book. The chapters are mostly short stories that convey some of my life experiences.

You will probably find them hard to believe, but all of them are completely true.

My hope is that this book reaches all four corners of the earth and that you, the reader will find it interesting and helpful, especially if you've ever wondered what this life is about and have asked yourself –

"Is there more to life than meets the eye?"

"Is the spirit realm real?"

If so, I hope my book can open your eyes a little.

It's just how it is

I was born in 1970, into a life that was not easy for me. I often felt fearful and sad growing up and my childhood was mostly unhappy. As a result, from the age of 15 I began to binge drink and this has led to a life-long battle with alcoholism.

I studied Chinese Medicine from the age of 19 and four years later at the age of 23 became a qualified Doctor of Chinese Medicine and a registered Acupuncturist.

I did well for myself financially and enjoyed a good lifestyle that included sports such as horse-riding, boating, fishing, and scuba-diving. I also enjoyed some snow-skiing and water-skiing.

I purchased my own home at the age of 28 and moved my Acupuncture Practice from a town office to my home, half of which was converted into a clinic for my work.

I had regarded my life as not being easy and a struggle, up until the age of 29. However, from age 30 until 45 my life dramatically worsened and became 'The Perfect Storm' the darkest winter of my life.

At age 30, soon after a botched surgery, I had a mental breakdown and a psychosis, leaving me terrified of living for a long period of time. This led to years of suffering and had such a snowball effect that I lost my partner, my home and my career – in fact everything that really mattered.

My life became one of mental distress, emotional pain and financial poverty. I lost the independence and security of owning my own home. My income protection insurance did not pay out because of a non-disclosure about a blood test result that I was not even aware of. I could no longer afford any of my recreational activities or lifestyle that I had been used to enjoying.

Here I am now, at 46 years of age, in 2017, as I write this book and finally good things have begun to happen. Things that have made my life so different than the one I will be telling you about.

It has come about only through my accepting Christianity. I was recently baptised with the Holy Spirit and am now fully devoted to God and to Jesus and trying to become the best man I possibly can as a son of God.

I have also stopped drinking and smoking and have at last found peace again in my life. I am no longer suffering any longer and am feeling upbeat, and hopefully my destitute financial situation will start to improve as well.

I hope that sharing my strange life experiences will open your eyes and get you thinking with an open mind. And that if you haven't already done so, to truly find God and not be like me and have one foot in and one foot out, up until the age of 45.

We can find the true path and plan that God has for us. It does us no good to believe in God, but only half-heartedly and neglect having a daily relationship with God and Jesus. Nor is it right to justify behaviour that is not God's will.

I've believed in God since I was about seven years old and have had many spiritual and supernatural experiences in my life. In this book you are about to read, you will discover a world that is beyond your wildest dreams, yet is real. This is why I titled the book "Spirit Realm - the Reality."

I don't know why I have had so many powerful spiritual experiences. I've never been perfect, and you will see in this book how I would try to work on myself spiritually in some areas, yet neglect to do so in others.

I feel that God wants me to write this book and share my life experiences with all who are willing to open their eyes and their minds and their hearts. Recently, at Stepping Stone Ministries for rehabilitation, I was praying and asking God about my book and would He and Jesus help me write it.

I immediately had a powerful experience of the Holy Spirit. This assured me that God did want me to write this book for mankind.

I do realise that many people will find what is written in my book hard to believe, and many will not believe it at all. But everything in my book is the truth, the whole truth, and nothing but the truth, so help me God.

Some of the accounts in my book contain extraordinary spiritual experiences, and some stories don't appear to include the spirit realm. However for me, all my experiences have aroused in me faith that God our Father and Jesus Christ love me and are helping me. This has brought me peace, strength, courage and a level, calm mind that has allowed me to make good and rational decisions in extremely dangerous, life-threatening moments.

Whenever danger is present, I always feel an unusual sense of peace, where I feel that many others would panic or crumble. God gives us power to overcome and to be victorious.

Glory be to God our Father and praise the Lord Jesus my Saviour.

God bless you all and my best wishes for you in believing and finding your true path and destiny to Eternal Life.

My encounter with Jesus

One day, when I was 25 I felt really unwell. I had been drinking the day before and on the Sunday was very hungover, even more so than usual. My thought was that I had alcohol poisoning. So I rang a Christian couple I knew and asked them if I could come over and visit them, and would they pray for my healing.

We began with a cup of tea together and then it was time for my healing session. So I lay on their massage table and relaxed and closed my eyes as they began to pray. I prayed along with them.

I then clearly saw in my mind what appeared to be a round pond. As I looked, something like a stone landed in it, causing ripples for a second or two. Then Jesus appeared in the pond. He tapped the palm of his left hand and pointed right at me. This filled me with a most wonderful, strong and powerful feeling. Jesus tapped his left hand again and pointed at me again with his right hand and once more I found myself experiencing the powerful feeling, even stronger than before. Then he did it a third time and I again felt his presence, his power and his love. This third time it was so intense I felt like I was one with God and one with Jesus.

The woman by my side praying, burst out crying and said several times, she was seeing Jesus, so I was not the only one that could see him. He had on a robe, long wavy hair and a beard plus brown moustache. He looked to be in his thirties, very much the same as we see him in the movies.

Not long after, I got off the massage table, feeling completely different. It was so amazing. I no longer felt unwell or hungover – instead I had a fantastically wonderful feeling of peace and joy.

I felt I had truly been touched by Jesus and said thank you to Jesus and felt another wave of his presence, also known as the Holy Spirit – it was very pleasant indeed. So for me, at age 25, I found out that Jesus is real and very much alive Powerful too, in the unseen spiritual realm.

Growing up

In the early years of my life I grew up as a little boy in Australia. I went to boy scouts and played football. I felt from a young age that I had a gift and I thought of myself as having powers and believed they would grow stronger in time. I started going to church at the age of 6.

My sister Adele was born when I was 10 and the following year our family moved to live here in New Zealand. We lived in Auckland for a few years.

I had a pony named Chamual, which I shared with my other sister Madeline. He was a fine-looking pony with a lovely nature, once I had broken him in. Madeline would ride him at the pony club. I loved riding him through the bush tracks.

For extra feed I would graze him in long grass at the rear of the cemetery, tied to a rope attached to a stake hammered into the ground. I also had other places I would stake him out to feed. Dad would sometimes send me out at night to retrieve Chamual from the back of the cemetery. I was not scared doing this alone, even though it was a little spooky.

I went to Sea Scouts and learned how to sail boats and became a group leader with a patrol under me. I also played rugby at school.

I worked for my father doing water blasting of drive-ways and houses. We would also spray chemicals on roofs to kill moss and sometimes we spray painted the roofs. The chemicals made the roof slippery and I slid down the roof and nearly fell off a couple of times.

My father did fall from a two-story roof one day. I was below operating the pump. He landed with his head nose down on the tar-seal in a pool of blood. I could tell by the sound of his breathing he was not getting much air. I knew that you're not supposed to move someone in case of causing paralysis but I made the choice to move his head and apparently that saved his life.

He was immediately placed in intensive care and had rods fitted to his legs and arms and a plate in his pelvis. He also sustained a head injury and once he recovered, it seemed hard for him to show me as much love as before and to have nice conversations with me. At that age I could not understand why my father did not love me as much as before, especially as he was a leader of the church he was involved in. One of the consequences is that I've not cried since I was about 13 years old, apart from one little tear after my brother Gabriel took his own life at the age of 23 (when I was 39.) I do feel emotional pain, but cannot cry, which is a sad situation in itself for me.

Anyway, one good thing was that by working for my father I saved up enough money to purchase a small Viking sail boat, and this led to me having more boats later in life.

From an early age I had always wanted an air rifle. When I was about 14 I was finally allowed one. I would shoot targets and cans and sparrows and so on. After a little while of this, I decided I did not want to shoot nice birds and that I would instead hunt myna birds, which are a relative of the magpie but a lot smaller. They raid other bird's nests, destroying their eggs and young. I enjoyed hunting them, because I would think of the harm they do, and it inspired me to keep hunting and shooting them. They would nest in the bush of an evening so I would head out to hunt them before the sun went down. I shot many mynas –17 in one night was my best tally.

I went on to do some pig hunting, possum and rabbit shooting. However, I did not do much hunting at all after reaching 20, as by then I felt compassion for the animals, even though they might be vermin. I am now a great lover of animals. I feed the sparrows and love dogs, cats and horses, not to mention the rest of the animal kingdom.

I have a son named Luke. He's a keen hunter and as good a shot as his father is.

Drilling for water

I was born in Perth, Western Australia, but both my parents were born in New Zealand. They moved to Perth after they married and it was there that I was conceived, and as mentioned earlier, our family moved back to New Zealand when I was 11 years old.

In this first story I'm still a young boy in Perth, not sure how old I was, maybe 7. My father, and his friend who lived across the road, had decided to dig for water. One bore was to be at our house and the other across the road.

We were digging the well across the road. One person would dig and the others would lift buckets of dirt out of the hole with a rope. As the hole got deeper, a large concrete ring was put in place. Then more digging, so that the concrete ring would slide down into the hole of the well. The bore well was getting rather deep and it was almost deep enough. There were now about five or six concrete rings in the well shaft, stacked on top of one another.

On this particular day, Dad was at the bottom of the well, about 40 feet down, digging. I was leaning over the side of the well and looking down. I had my hands on the edge of the concrete ring when suddenly the concrete rings slid down.

Over the edge I went and almost fell all the way down, head first, 40 feet. Luckily I had fast reflexes and quickly grabbed the top edge of the concrete ring. So there I was, hanging upside down with my feet up in the air. My helmet fell off and hit Dad on his head and he looked up to see me hanging there. The men that were there were laughing at me, and after waiting a few moments, which felt like eternity, one of them grabbed my ankles and pulled me to safety. Whew!

Hunting for gold

When I was about 8 years old I tried prospecting for gold, not with a metal detector but dowsing with two lengths of wire. I was very successful at this.

My parents would hide gold rings in the grass and sand, and then send me out to find and retrieve them. Off I would go with my divining rods, my two lengths of wire bent over on the ends for a handle. When I passed over where the gold was hidden, the rods would cross over, indicating that the gold was right there. I would check it again just to make sure. Then I would find the gold in the very spot where the rods crossed over each other.

We sometimes went on an adventure into the outback and we would hunt for gold. Dad had a metal detector and I had my rods. One time we planned to do two trips to the Australian outback. On the first one, we got about 50 km past a town named Sandstone when our 4-wheel drive Toyota Landcruiser broke down – the rear diff had seized up.

We waited all day long in the heat for the sight of another vehicle. There was a dead bull lying on the road nearby and someone had told the local sheriff about it a few days earlier. Fortunately, he chose this very day to drive out to look at it, and stumbled across us while he was doing so, thank goodness.

He gave us a ride back to Sandstone, where we went to the pub. I had lemon lime and bitters with lemonade. We shacked up for the night in an abandoned railway shed. Dad had arranged with a truck driver who was drinking at the bar to load our Landcruiser on his trailer and take us back to Perth. However, the truck driver still had to deliver his load and would come back for us in a couple of days. So we carried on looking for gold.

We hadn't found much gold worth mentioning, but my dowsing rods did lock onto a good spot to dig, and we dug a hole. Dad ran his metal detector over the hole and it signalled gold was under the ground, so we kept digging and sifting sand and dirt through a sifting ring that leaves the nuggets on the mesh. Then a 4-wheel drive pulled up and a man claimed we were on leased gold mining land and we needed to move on immediately. I was peeved off as I had had my heart set on a big gold nugget and we had already found that special spot.

Well, the truck driver came back for us and we jumped in his truck and headed out of Sandstone to get our Landcruiser. We found a dirt loading ramp left from miners not far from our truck, so with Landcruiser's rear wheels still locked-up, we drove it and got towed by the truck to the ramp. Then we winched our vehicle up onto the truck trailer.

The truck was an 18 speed Mack and the truck driver drove at about 130kph (80mph) on the dirt roads on the way back to Perth. In the process my bull terrier called Sundowner was injured when he fell off the back of the truck and got dragged for some time before we noticed. So I had to patch him up when we got home.

A month later we headed back into the outback. This time we left my dog at home recovering and took along a young man named John. He had tattoos and was a recovering drug addict who went to our church, so Dad invited him to come along.

It is dangerous out in the desert. Abandoned mine shafts are here and there with no warning of them and they were very deep, dropping straight down. If you did not look where you were walking you could fall to your death. I sat at the edge of a few of them and dropped rocks down and would count until I heard them hit the bottom. One morning I awoke and found a dugite snake about six feet long slithering over me, so I lay very still as their bite is deadly.

Dad said the trip cost him more than the amount of gold we found, but it was an adventure to remember.

As a young boy I firmly believed I had spiritual powers, and if you truly believe such things are possible then supernatural powers and experiences will develop and grow in you.

I now know that if you trust and have faith that God will protect you, then He does exactly that.

Hallelujah! Amen.

I can't find my watch

When I was 10 years old, I went with my family to visit and stay with my uncle and aunt. At some stage I realised I had lost my watch and went looking for it. I looked everywhere but couldn't find it.

We were leaving the next day, so I prayed for God's angels to help me find it. That night I had a dream that I walked over to one of the couches in the lounge, dug my hand into it behind and under the cushions and pulled out my watch.

In the morning I was woken up by my parents saying, "Hurry and get up, we have to go now!" Then I remembered my dream, so I ran over to the couch in the lounge, dug my hand down behind the cushions and on the first attempt found myself grabbing hold of something. I pulled it out and it was my watch! I didn't even have to slide my hand along to find it.

That is why I believe God was allowing his angels to help me find my watch that day.

What a ride!

Now I have fallen off my bike plenty of times, but this time it was different. When I was nearly 11, a spiritual woman said to me during communion at church one day, that she had a message for me. The message was, "Tomorrow, or sometime soon, you will crash off your bike. But before you leave home you will sense something is wrong and decide to put on safety gear that includes a jacket, gloves and a helmet."

Well, one night many months later, when I decided to ride my bike to visit a friend, I sensed something was wrong and was worried I would have a crash. I also remembered the woman that told me I would fall off my bike one day. So I went and found my army jacket that I hardly ever wore, got some gloves and a helmet and put them on.

Off I went into the night, at high speed down the steep long hill leaving my house. At the bottom was a slab of broken concrete lying in the middle of the road that I could not see. I hit it and came down with a terrible crash on the road and nearly lost consciousness. I rolled over into the gutter so cars would not run me over and just lay there. I had skin missing on my hands and face and elbows and knees. I was so grateful I had taken the time to put on some safety gear.

After some time, I managed to get up and get my bike. I was surprised that several cars had just driven past. They just drove around my bike and did not seem to care if I was hurt. I checked my bike and it was badly damaged – the wheels were buckled and the handle bars bent. So I just walked to my friend's house, pushing it. My head was not good either as I had concussion.

I had sensed something was wrong before I left on my ride and decided to put on that safety gear. It's a good idea to follow your gut feeling on things. And as I said, I believed I had a gift from a young age and as I would later discover, it grew and developed as I got older. Believing and faith are the keys to developing a gift like I have.

Electrocuted in America

When we left Australia when I was 11, we lived in Los Angeles for three months before coming to New Zealand. Dad took us to America first, as he wanted to study at a church he was involved in. I attended a Montessori school for those three months.

I went camping with the kids and won first prize for building the best and biggest campfire. The bush was wet, so it was a mission and we had to start the fire the old-fashioned way. We had no matches so I rolled a stick between my hands on another piece of wood, creating the friction needed to start my fire.

Towards the end of our time in America, we went and stayed with some people at their house. I went out in the garden where there was a swimming pool, and next to the house was a stainless steel water filter. I was interested in this filter and wanted to look inside it. It had a handle on either side of it, so I grabbed them both.

Suddenly I found myself convulsing, shuddering and shaking with electric current surging through my body. I could not open my hands to let go of the filter as they were clamped hard on to the handles – I was in real trouble. I tried to call out for help but couldn't say a word. I realized I was going to die if the electricity was not shut down quickly.

In my mind I was praying to God for help. Through a window I could see my father sitting at a table inside the house, but he was not looking at me. I was praying in my mind, "Come on Dad, look at me! Shut the power off".

After about 30 seconds of being electrocuted, Dad looked out at me for about 10 seconds before realising what was happening. Then he got up and ran. I was elated, thinking "Yes, he's going to save me." But about another 15 seconds passed by and I was still shuddering with the current surging through me. My jaw was clamped shut fast as well as my hands on the water filter. Then suddenly the power was shut off at last. Oh the relief that I had been saved and was still alive. It must have been only about a minute that I was being electrocuted, but it felt a whole lot longer. I was truly grateful that Dad had saved me.

Glory be to God. Halleluiah, Amen!

Doubles on the bike

I was now 12 and living in Auckland. One day as I was walking home, my friend Carl stopped alongside me on his push bike and offered me a ride home, down the long steep hill that I lived on.

He said he would double me, so I sat on the horizontal bar that runs between the handle bars and the seat, then the two of us set off down the big hill – Carl on the bike seat and me sitting sideways on the cross bar.

There we were, zooming down Eskdale Road hill at top speed. It was raining and the road was very wet. As we got close to my house, Carl began to steer his bike across to the other side of the road. Then suddenly a car came speeding around the corner heading in our direction. Carl braked hard, but the tyres locked up and we started to skid sideways, and then went right around in a circle, skidding a whole 360 degrees and came to a stop as the tyre bumped into the curb. The car just avoiding running us over. I remember clearly it was a blue Volkswagen and after just missing us, revved its engine and sped off.

Thank goodness we stayed on the bike and did not fall off into the path of the speeding car.

I believe that was because God was still looking after me, and he did it well. Amen!

The angel who helped

This next experience happened when I was 18 and on a working holiday in Perth, Western Australia.

I had made two friends and they wanted me to go for a drive with them. So I got in the car, sitting in the front passenger seat and we pulled out of the driveway.

Then I heard a voice, which I believed was an angel. He said, "Adrian, put your belt on." So I thought, OK I will do that and I put my seat belt on. Then I said, "Thank you for that," and right away I felt a nice wave of the Holy Spirit wash over me.

The three of us started to drive off down the road, and then Shane, in the back seat said, "Hey, how does your new car handle?" The next thing I know the car is surging forward, accelerating at great speed down the road. Then we made a left turn and back to speeding down the road again. We accelerated up to 170kms per hour (105mph) and we were approaching a double lane round-about.

The driver slowed the car down to about 120kph (75mph) just as we were about to enter it. When we were half way through it, the tyres began to squeal and the driver panicked. He slammed the brakes on hard, which locked up the tyres, causing the car to skid in a straight line instead of turning through the round-about. We skidded straight into the kerb and then launched up it, head-on into a power pole We smashed into it with a horrendous, jolting stop.

This punched the wind right out of me and I couldn't breathe and blacked out. I awoke soon after and could see steam or smoke coming from the front of the car. My two friends seemed to be conscious, from what I could see. I tried to open my car door, but it wouldn't budge, and neither would the driver's door. I looked at the speedometer and the needle was stuck on 110 km per hour. I said to the driver, "You kick my door while I hold the latch open." He moved himself around into a side-on position and kicked my door. It wasn't enough, so I said, "Kick it again, and again." Then it opened and I was able to get out of the vehicle.

"Thank goodness for that," I thought. I did not like being trapped inside the car as I was worried it might burst into flames. My knees were very sore where they had hit into the edge of the glove box. My shoulder was very sore from the seat belt and my neck did not feel good, but I was relieved to be alive.

I looked at the power pole, and saw just behind and to the side of it, a solid tree, and thought, "Gosh, with no belt on, if I had smashed through the windscreen, I might have also flown head on into the tree, causing more injury or death. Just the thought of smashing into the dashboard and going through the windscreen was bad enough.

I felt lucky to be alive and was grateful that the angel had seen what was about to happen and warned me to put on my seat belt. Someone surely was looking after me, and I believe it was God and the Lord Jesus and that angel.

So much to be grateful for

When I was 33, I was in an even more serious car accident. I had swerved to avoid a man standing in the middle of the road and my car crashed into the back of a truck parked on the side of the road.

I was doing over 50kph (30mph) , possibly as much as 70kph (45mph). I had no seat belt on and although I slammed the brakes on, I didn't have time to slow down much, then CRUNCH! I smashed into the back of the truck. I held onto the steering wheel so hard, it bent in like a banana and the steering column collapsed, with me launching up over it and my head smashing into the windscreen so hard I could literally hear my neck crunching.

Every inch of the windscreen was shattered and there was a bulge where my head had hit it. And right in front of the windscreen was the back of the truck deck – the front of my car had gone under the truck. I don't think I was far off going through the window and smacking into the rear of the truck.

I slumped back into my seat as blood was spurting out of me onto the windscreen and all over the place. I felt as if I was about to pass out. Someone came over asking if I was alright. I said, "No, I'm not too good." People tried to get me out of the car as they could smell petrol. Someone got my dog out of the back seat. She must have crashed into the back of the passenger seat hard, as afterwards they said she was struggling to walk and fell over.

The ambulance came and put me on a spinal board and took me to hospital. The doctor wondered why my chest was not sore and ribs were not bruised or broken. I said I held onto the steering wheel very tightly and sort of rose up over it into the windscreen. He said I will need x-rays and some stitches. I asked to use the phone and he unstrapped my hand to use it. After he walked off, I managed to loosen some straps that were holding me down and I took off the neck brace and walked out of the hospital. I just wanted to go home. I was alive and grateful for that, and that was good enough for me.

Several times I've nearly broken my neck or back in accidents out horse-riding. I sometimes wonder about the people that do simple things, like fall backwards off a lounge chair and break their necks, then have to get around in a wheelchair. A lot of people in this world don't get extra chances in life like I seem to.

This reminds me of my grandfather, who used to tell a story that I will share with you here about when he and Nana met.

Grandad was riding his Harley Davidson along a dirt farm road and Nana was coming from the other direction riding her horse, when they met suddenly on a corner. Grandad took evasive action and left the road on his bike, hurtling into a farm fence and flying through a prickle bush. He said later that he landed on his feet.

Nana went to his aid, taking him back to her home. There she hid him from her parents as she plucked all the prickles out of him. They later married.

Some people think Grandad is a great storyteller and just made up the part about landing on his feet. However, I tend to believe him, as I've fallen at speed and twice managed to land on my feet.

I often include in my prayers to the Lord some thank you prayers, in gratefulness for being alive and not in a wheelchair. It's important to have gratitude. The Lord likes us to be grateful for what we do have, and not continually wanting things in our prayers. God hears us and often answers us too.

I believe one of the keys to successful prayer is to pray from our heart, and to be sincere and really mean what we are saying. I feel that this pleases the Lord.

Is this party from heaven or from hell?

My first extremely powerful experience with God was at age 18. I was at a party and I had not been there long. I was drinking my first beer and had not been taking drugs.

Someone came up to me and said, "You had better get out of here as someone is planning to stab you." I felt very concerned.

As I needed to go to the bathroom to relieve myself, I headed there first instead of to the exit and I started to pray. I prayed to God, Jesus and the angels. After using the toilet, I spent a while longer in prayer and then felt faith arise in me that God would help me.

As I left the bathroom, I turned the palms of my hands upward, as one does in worship and took a few steps towards the door to leave. But as soon as I turned my hands upward, I was filled with the Holy Spirit which felt extremely strong, and got even more so. I felt as if I was one with God – as if I was directly connected to him.

Suddenly I could hear people yelling loudly, "It's the light! Run! Get out of here!" This was repeated several times by people and they were running past me, heading for the door. Two of them jumped over the balcony rails, as the outside stairs were blocked with people running from the house. In all, about a dozen people fled the house and up the driveway, crossed the road and gathered there.

I too went outside and stood on the lawn, while several others gathered around me. They asked me things like, "How did you do that?" and "That was amazing!" And that they had never felt like that before, or seen anything like it before, and asked if I could do it again.

I said, "No, that was God not me." A woman asked again can you do it again, so I repeated, "No, it was God and he was just using me as a tool to do that."

I was told that the ones that fled the house were members of a satanic cult and obviously could not handle the experience

24

very well at all. The ones that didn't run had a lovely experience and felt God.

Sometimes you hear people say, "I pray, but God does not answer my prayers." It might seem that way, yet sometimes God will answer our prayer immediately if he decides to do so. And a spiritual experience can be so powerful it's beyond your wildest dreams.

Do not give up.

Knife attack

This experience next took place when I was 19, in a house where my girlfriend Jody was working as a nanny and living there with the family she was working for.

I had gone over to visit her and to stay a couple of days. Jill, a good friend of Jody was also living there in the same house, as they enjoyed each other's company.

Jody had befriended a young man who wanted us both to go out go-cart racing, so we did just that. Then he wanted to have drinks with me alone, so we bought a bottle of Jim Beam from the store and went back to Jody's place. While we were drinking, he told stories of his gang life and his addiction to hard drugs and heroin.

What I was unaware of, was that Jody had been sleeping with him. After more drinking, he became nasty and started talking tough. Then he began to threaten me and wanted me to go outside for a fight. However, once I was standing outside facing him ready to fight, he backed down, not wanting to fight me.

We went back inside and consumed more whisky for a while, then he got up and walked out of the room down to Jill's bedroom, where the two girls where. I heard him saying things like,

"Do you want him or me?"

A short time after that I heard him say, "I'm going to get a knife and I'm going to kill him."

I decided to take him seriously, so I got up and walked out the back door that was not far from the table we had been drinking at. I stood to the side of the doorway up against the wall. I thought I would wait for him to find me. I could hear him calling out my name. I waited in silence and felt it would not be long before he came outside looking for me.

The next thing I spotted was the knife coming out the door as he was holding it in front of him. I grabbed his wrist then pushed on his back with my other hand and bent his arm up behind his back. I told him to drop the knife but he did not and instead raved on, abusing me. So I bent his arm up some more and he dropped it. I let him go only to have him attack me by throwing a punch. I responded by blocking it and then punched him back. He fell to the ground after my first punch, unconscious.

I picked up the knife and chose to not kick or harm him, but just leave him lying on the driveway. I took the knife inside and told Jody and Jill what had just happened and that they better not let him back inside. Then I sat and had another drink. After about half an hour I walked outside and found he had gone.

Later I found out that Jody was pregnant at the time of this incident. Thank goodness I was not murdered that day, as it was my child she was carrying. My son Luke has grown up having a father. He is now 25 and married and I am a proud grandfather.

Thanks be to God!

Do we have a soul?

At age 22 I was studying Chinese medicine and acupuncture. One night I was fast asleep and I was woken up because I heard a noise. The part that is unusual about this night, is that when I sat up, I realised that my body was still asleep on the bed and I was looking down at my head on the pillow.

This did not worry or frighten me, I just thought "Wow, this is bizarre. I'm out of my body," and wondered whether I would go somewhere or just stay there.

I decided I would stay put and went to lay back down into my body. It felt different than it usually does to lie down. It felt like I was going down very slowly like a hydraulic machine would move – it was slow and smooth. I suppose that's because there is no body weight involved in the movement.

The next morning I told my girlfriend Jody and my mother about it, and how it was an amazing experience.

I now relate a similar experience I had a few years later when I was 25. I was fast asleep when I found myself flying up above my house and then up higher into the air. I then flew for a few kilometres. I could see my arms stretched out as I was flying and I could tell they were in spirit form and not flesh and bone. I found myself stopping way up in the air above Lake Rotorua and I could see Mokoia Island in the middle of it. I could also see the moonlight shining on the water. I was about 150 metres or more up above the lake and from that position I could see many city lights in the distance. Then I decided I wanted to go home and started moving again, but much faster than before. It seemed I was controlling the flight with my mind.

But what is very interesting, is that about two years later, the day before my 27th birthday, I blew up the V8 motor in my boat and it sank in the very spot on Lake Rotorua that I saw below in my flight in my spirit body.

So, why did my spirit fly up and look down on the exact location of the boating accident well before it happened? Only God knows.

Man overboard

I enjoy sailing, having gone to Sea Scouts as a boy. I had my own little 9-foot yacht that I worked and saved up for. I would also go out sailing on my friend Carl's, family 25-foot yacht.

Years later, at the age of 27 I drove to Auckland to go sailing with Carl on his 18-foot bilge keeler. Things started off fine and we were both enjoying the day. It was the afternoon by now and the water was very choppy and rough.

We had consumed quite a lot of beer during the day and were headed home, sailing with the wind behind us. Carl had gone inside the cabin to use his phone. The boat was rocking a fair bit from the very big choppy sea. I decided to get myself a can of beer, so I stood up as the beer was stored under one of the boat's seats, and in so doing so I fell overboard.

As I fell, I grabbed one of the main sheet ropes on my way into the water. I found myself being dragged along beside the boat with my face crashing into the choppy waves.

I had to time my breathing and hold my breath. I waited and waited for Carl to get off his phone and come out of the cabin. My arms were getting tired from holding on, as there was a lot of drag from crashing through the choppy sea.

Two minutes passed, then I heard Carl calling out my name. I yelled and he looked over the side of the boat and saw me in the water being towed along. It was a bit of a mission to get me back on-board but once I was sitting there, I was so relieved and grateful that I was safe and alive.

If I had not been able to grab the rope that was dangling over the water running between the boom and the boat on my way overboard, I would have been left swimming in the choppy water with no life jacket and would soon have been drowned in the water.

Being half drunk I would not have been able to swim very long in those very choppy conditions. In addition, Carl would have had to discover he had a man overboard then turn the boat around and tack up wind looking for me in choppy water. This would have taken at least ten minutes and I would be dead long before he found me.

Only God knows why he has allowed me more than nine lives. Praise the Lord. Amen!

Horses are special

Horses are lovely animals. I got my first pony at age 12 and loved riding – it felt like I was getting back to nature. I also liked the feeling that men have been riding horses for thousands of years and it really wasn't all that long ago that cars took their place in the area of transport.

Now my first pony Chamual was a lovely looking New Forest breed pony. He was at first unbroken and it was a challenge breaking him in, but I learnt the importance of getting back on a horse right away after you have fallen off. I would ride him through forest tracks in the area we lived.

At age 15 I moved with my family to Rotorua and then stopped horse riding until I was 23. Then I began riding again after my Acupuncture and Chinese Medicine study was nearly complete. This time I rode ex-race horses and my main horse was named Zaddy. He was difficult to ride as he was explosive in power and speed and would fizz, that is, 'go nutty'. This was especially so on the hunting field, galloping along with the other horses, where he acted like he was racing them.

I enjoyed the hunt, which is a traditional old English sport. You have a pack of hounds and follow them on horseback as they chase their prey to kill it. In New Zealand the hounds hunt down hares, which are much larger and faster than rabbits, but look similar. It's a fun and fast-paced sport when the chase is on, and we would hurdle the farm fences as we rode across farmland.

I rode this wild racehorse of mine with faith that God was with me, especially as I would come crashing off my horse many times, sometimes with nasty injuries. I've fallen off horses over 25 times and have had close calls with almost breaking my back and neck. Thank goodness I'm OK and alive to tell the story.

On one hunt I was having a good afternoon, enjoying jumping the farm fences as I rode Zaddy down a hillside. At the bottom of this hill was a farm fence made of tightly strung, high tensile steel wire. We were cantering down this hill and approaching this fence when Zaddy got in too close to the fence to jump it properly. Nevertheless he did jump and caught his front legs on the wire.

This sent me hurtling forward and I lost my seat and fell off, landing on the ground with a thud and then heard the snapping of the high tensile wires. This sounded like two shots from a .22 rifle.

I was worried my horse would fall down and crush me, all 500 kilograms of him, but he didn't fall and landed on his feet. However, his hoof hit my neck, bruising and damaging it and putting it out of place. Then he raced off across to the next paddock.

Normal farm fences are made of 8 gauge wire or barbed wire, so they stretch and move and only sometimes break. The horse usually will flip over the fence and crash land and can crush and kill the rider. I was very lucky my horse did not break my neck on this occasion or even kill me.

Some riders went off chasing my horse to catch him, while I laid on the ground, stunned from the impact, with my neck very sore from the horse's hoof.

I am very grateful to have survived and be OK. If the horse's hoof had come down on me one inch more to the left, I would be dead or in a wheelchair drinking from a straw.

Thank you God that I'm walking around today.

More hunting happenings

The hunt is an exciting and exhilarating sport, but there's more to it than meets the eye. There's the feeding of the horses and making sure they have water for example. There's also lots of exercising of the horses outside of the hunt season, and all the other things to do when you own horses.

One afternoon, my father Neil and I loaded the horses on our truck and took them to the beach for exercise. It was raining heavily that day, and by the time we got to the beach the sea was rough with large waves. We went galloping along the beach for a few kilometres and then walked the horses for a while. Normally we would walk them in the water but the waves were too big that day.

On the way back to the truck we had broken into a fast gallop and Zaddy was really going for it. I could not see much as the rain was heavy and my glasses were wet. Even if I hadn't had my glasses on, my vision would have been poor.

We were galloping along at about 65kph (40mph) when Zaddy suddenly jumped violently sideways, throwing me off, as he'd just come across a dead sheep that had been washed up. I came crashing down on my neck and shoulder and my back arched and bent the wrong way and felt a lot of pain. Zaddy continued to gallop off along the hard sand on the beach.

I lay on the hard sand for a while, flat on my back in agony, thinking I had broken my back. But I could still move my fingers and toes and was grateful I wasn't paralysed. After a while I got up and walked slowly and painfully back to the horse truck. I found Zaddy and my father waiting for me next to it.

I said to my father, "I think I've broken my back."

He said "It won't be broken if you are walking around as you are." I felt he was wrong. Even though I wasn't paralysed, I felt like it was partially broken.

Acupuncture was helpful for awhile, but about six months or so later I went to see a chiropractor because of the on-going pain. He took x-rays and told me that I really had broken my back. He said that I should have spent three months in hospital in traction – that is, held in a fixed position and rotated around all the time.

Well, I was grateful that I was still walking around and not in a wheel chair considering what the chiropractor had diagnosed. He also told me, that any time since the accident while I had been walking around, I could have complicated the injury and become paralysed, leaving me in a wheel chair. However it was too late to put me in traction as a lot of healing had already taken place. Nevertheless, it still took seven years for the pain to completely go away.

What I had was a 25% compression fracture and a wedge fracture on my lumbar 1 and thoracic 12 vertebrae. I still have trouble with my spine going out and I partially click it in place a few times a day myself by bending my back sideways. Chiropractic treatment now and then is helpful as well.

About four years after that accident on the beach, I was out in the field riding in a hunt on a fine winter's day. I was riding a horse named Six Pack, a lovely horse and a pleasure to ride as he was well-behaved and easy to control. He was one of my friend Bill's horses.

I was enjoying the hunt and the chase was on. I was following the hounds as they were in pursuit of a hare. As I was galloping along this paddock and approaching a farm fence, I could see a dog sitting next to it. I did not know why it was there, or if it had been tied up to the fence. (I would later find out that the farmer had tied his dog there as a deterrent to stop people from jumping the fence at that point as there was a tightly strung wire going from the fence on an angle up to the top of a pole.)

I could not see the wire and did not realise that there was a serious hazard ahead. I manoeuvred the horse so he would approach the fence well over to the right of the dog. We galloped into the fence and Six Pack launched up into the air. At the last moment I saw the wire and in a fraction of a second ducked my head and whole body down onto the horse's neck. Just at that moment I felt the wire scrape over my helmet making a twanging noise. If I had not reacted so rapidly I would have had my throat cut all the way to my vertebrae, or my whole head simply cut right off.

Thank God I'm alive to tell that story.

I am convinced that if you truly believe in God and have faith in him he helps things work out for the better and helps you stay alive.

See Psalm 91 in the Old Testament regarding this.

Riding for a fall or two

I was 24. It was a fine winter's day and the hunt was nearly over.

The hunt would usually start at noon and finish at 3pm, sometimes a bit later if there is a chase on with the hounds. There was a bit of a queue waiting for a particular jump – it was a full, seven wire fence. My horse Zaddy hated waiting and was turning circles and walking sideways with anticipation and adrenalin flowing.

Then a gap opened up and I let Zaddy go. He spun around, faced the fence and exploded in power, flicking mud up in the air as he raced to the fence to jump it. (I used to call him Road Runner as he was so fast, both on take-off and in galloping.) We galloped at high speed to the fence and he jumped – but he judged it wrong. His front hooves hit the top wire of the fence and I heard the sound this makes, alerting me we were in for a crash. I flicked my heels back to get free of my stirrups. As I started to launch off my horse, I spread my arms out to fly. I landed tucked into a ball and held my helmet with my hands, rolling three times then popping up to land on my feet. The crowd cheered and clapped for me.

Zaddy flipped head over heels and crashed down on his head and neck. It took him a while to get to his feet and he had a blood nose and couldn't walk properly. I had a sore ankle and was a bit sore in other places, but was good considering the crash we'd just had. I decided not to climb back on my horse as I would usually do, in my concern for Zaddy. I walked him back to the truck. My hip flask in the pocket of my saddle blanket was completely crushed from his weight rolling over it.

I was grateful I was able to divest myself of my stirrups, thereby getting a clear exit from my 500kg horse. I would not have enjoyed ending up under that weight for sure.

The other hunting fall I recall was rather similar, which occurred a few years later when I was 29. I was riding a lovely mare called Novar who was 16.1 hands (1.6m/5.4ft) high. It was another nice fine winters day and Novar had been going well, but she was starting to get a little tired. We had been on some long, fast runs and they had taken some of the zest out of her. We were waiting at a jump as there was a pile-up of horses and riders waiting to jump this fence. Novar was getting impatient, champing at the bit and prancing around, rearing to go. I saw a gap open and let her go for it. She raced to the fence eagerly. Then I noticed that two other riders had let their horses go at the same time, so there were three of us all racing for the same jump.

Almost at the last moment my horse veered out to the left, as we had been pushed out by another horse. We now had a problem – the position we had been pushed into wasn't very viable – there was a dug-out area just before the farm fence made by the farmer's cattle so it was going to be a very high, five-foot jump and we were committed to it and there wasn't enough room or time to pull out of it.

So, in we went at full gallop, and I heard the dreaded noise when a horse's front hooves get caught on the top wire of a fence. I kicked my heels back to drop the stirrups and off I went. I touched Novar's ear to say, "See you later," then spread my arms out for the flight. As I came down to crash land, I again tucked into a ball and rolled three times, then again popped up, landing on my feet. Again the crowd on their horses went wild, yelling out and clapping. I grabbed the tip of my helmet and bowed to them. It's a great feeling to end up standing on your feet after a big fast crash.

I was actually a bit concussed from the fall, but fine really. Novar flipped end-over-end and crashed, but was OK this time, though sadly, only three weeks later, someone else crashed her, jumping a farm fence and she needed to be put down for good.

A day out boating

It was a fine sunny day and two friends wanted to go out on my boat. So the three of us, Carl, Jeffery and myself, set off to do some water skiing on Lake Rotorua.

My boat was a 20 foot with a V8 motor and one of the guys was really keen to go out for his first time on my boat. However, on the way to the lake I began to feel uneasy. I said, "I don't feel good about this trip. Something's wrong. Let's go home and give it a miss today guys."

But they said, "No way" and made fun of me for being paranoid, so I went along with them.

Before starting the boat though, I gathered the life jackets and put them all together in one spot in the bow. I only had three life jackets, and had already that morning prevented two young lady friends from coming out on the boat that day because of that. My uneasy feeling lessened after I had taken that precaution. They would be there in case we needed them in a hurry.

The water was flat as a pancake, the water-skiing was under way and things were going fine. Then suddenly the boat broke down and stopped. We took the engine cover off and started to look into the problem and could smell petrol fumes. The day before, Carl and I had gone out water-skiing and the boat had conked out on us a few times. What Carl had not told me, was that while I was out sitting in the water on the ski's waiting for him to get the boat started again, he had been emptying the fuel bowl into the bilge of the boat.

Water from condensation formed in the fuel tanks had mixed with the petrol and built up in the fuel bowl on the motor. Carl had trouble removing the fuel bowl from the engine so he just emptied the water and fuel mix into the bilge. This meant that there was a build-up of petrol under the floor boards in the bottom of the boat and dangerous fumes had been evaporating from it.

So that was the situation we were now faced with. We tipped buckets of water into the bilge to dilute the petrol and turned the bilge pump on to pump the water and petrol out of the boat. We left the engine cover off to help the fumes escape and sat on the boat chatting and enjoying the sunshine as we had to waited quite a long time.

I noticed also, that the air filter on top of the motor was not fixed properly onto the motor and could see that the bolt to hold it in place was broken. This combination of problems with the boat was not good.

My phone rang. It was my friend Greg. He said he was standing on the jetty holding a tray of beer for me as it was my birthday the next day. I explained to him we had problems with the boat, but almost had it sorted and would make our way over to the jetty soon. So we decided to give the boat a try and I turned the key. It back-fired and flames shot out around the badly fitting air filter and ignited the fumes, causing an explosion. BOOM. I saw a large blue and yellow fireball of flames leaping up from the sides of the motor.

I went for the fire extinguisher and grabbed it from the bow. I wish I had grabbed the life jackets at the same time, but I didn't. Jeffery panicked and jumped overboard, leaping from the side of the boat, which made it rock. The boat rocking caused me to fall down beside the flames from the engine bay and the side wall of the boat. I reached up my arm holding the fire extinguisher so Carl could grab it.

He pulled the pin and blasted the flames, giving me a chance to get up and move away from them. I had to do it quickly as I could not see anything but white because of the fire extinguisher's white-out effect. Carl continued to blast the flames that were also emanating now from the sides of the floor boards and stern of the boat. I grabbed the auxiliary fuel tank and heaved it overboard.

The fire seemed to go out and there was a moment of relief. Then WOOF the fire erupted once again, but the fire extinguisher had by then run dry.

Carl asked, "What now?"

I said, "Walk up the side of the boat to the bow."

We stood up the front and looked through the sun roof at the flames roaring from the motor. The engine was still running. Carl then yelled, "I'm out of here!" and jumped into the water.

I looked from one side to the other and thought, "It's about three miles to shore either way and the water is cold." So I decided the only way to survive was to get the life jackets. I smashed at the Perspex plastic window so I could get into the front cabin of the boat. I smashed at the window six or seven times until I had made a hole big enough for me to enter the boat. I climbed in and went for the life jackets. I found two but could not see or feel the third one as there was a lot of black smoke, and also the hole I had come in through was creating a vacuum and sucking flames to it. I finally managed to find the third jacket, but by this time I had taken a couple of breaths of toxic black air and was starting to feel light-headed and struggling not to cough. I looked at the window, my only way out, yet the flames were now roaring out that window. But I was determined to live and survive, so I put my feet up onto the window ledge, shielding the flames with the life jackets, and started to edge my way out. It was not easy. I held the jackets with one hand, held myself up with my other hand and started working my way out backwards.

Sharp edges on the broken window cut into me and also snagged on my clothing, but I managed to get out and stand up on the front of the boat. The jackets were on fire, so I hurled them out to the men in the water, thinking the water would put them out. But they floated on the water with some flames still coming off them. My hair had been on fire and most of it was burnt, as were my eyebrows. I jumped into the water and struggled to put my jacket on. It was difficult to do in the water. I thought I should have put it on before I jumped from the boat, but just as well I didn't, for soon after I jumped, one of the two petrol tanks exploded, blasting the flames everywhere and a massive fireball erupted.

If I had taken one minute longer to get into the boat and retrieve the jackets, I would have not made it out alive, not to mention that burning is a horrible way to die.

While floating in the water I could feel the heat on my face and felt that I must swim away from the boat. The guys in the water watching had been saying, that when I was inside the boat they were looking at each other yelling, "Look at the flames leaping out the window. There's no way Adrian's getting out alive."

Then BOOM the second fuel tank exploded and another huge fireball erupted and flames danced on the water as a really big mushroom cloud rose into the sky. The top of the boat and the cabin had been blown off and bits of the boat were on fire. Then there was a fourth explosion – it was the spare fire extinguisher, which blew a hole in the side of the boat and flew like a missile through the air.

The heat was now burning my face and I had to swim further and further from the inferno. The guys then began singing, 'Happy Birthday' to me, as it was my birthday the following day. Funnily enough, my birthday is on Guy Fawkes day (the 5th November) the day where fireworks are let off in New Zealand.

We floated in the water and waited for help. We did some swimming, but as it was early November and the water was still at its chilly winter temperature. Our teeth began to chatter as we shivered and huddled together in an attempt to slow down hypothermia.

It was half an hour before a jet boat came to our rescue. They had seen a big mushroom cloud in the sky over the lake, so headed over to investigate.

A boat plane landed on the water as well and took a photo that was on the front page of the local newspaper the following day.

As the jet boat was approaching, Jeffery got excited and started yelling out. He also pushed down on my shoulder as he was waving out to the jet boat. This shoved me under the water and I had to punch at him to get him to release me from his grasp. Then suddenly my body went limp on one side and I could not speak, except for some mumbo jumbo sounds. I thought, "This can't be happening. Have I had a stroke? Will this be the last day of my life as I know it?"

The jet boat pulled alongside us and helped pull the other two in. Then they came to help me, but had to literally lift me into the boat as I was paralysed down one side. I flopped onto the floor of the boat and they just left me lying there.

I managed to splutter out some words saying, "Put me on the seat." They lifted me up onto the seat and off we went at full speed, heading for the shore.

I hung my head out over the side of the boat as it was easier to breathe with the wind blasting on my face and my breathing was not good. However on the trip back to shore, my arm and leg started to improve and miraculously came right. So I was able to walk along the jetty by myself to shore. There was an ambulance waiting and lots of tourists standing on the lake edge, clapping their hands as we walked to the ambulance.

I asked for an oxygen mask but the ambulance officer did not think I needed it. A policeman began asking me questions like, "How long was my boat?" and "What happened?" Then, still gasping for air, I collapsed. I woke up later on the way to hospital with an oxygen mask on my face. Sometime later the doctor said we all had hypothermia but they weren't sure yet why I had become temporarily paralysed.

They wanted me to stay until I was medically cleared to go home. However, I was keen to leave and my friend Greg had come to see if I was OK. So I said to him, "Bring your concrete truck up outside the hospital entrance, I'm going to do a runner to escape." So I waited a few minutes, then got up and made my way to the hospital entrance, walked out, jumped into his truck and away we went.

We drove back to my house and sat outside in the sun to warm up, and drank some Steinlager, the beer Greg had bought for me. We heard over the radio in a news report that three men were lucky to survive after blowing up their boat on Lake Rotorua. We said to each other, "Wow, that's us!" and chatted away about how fortunate we were to be alive, sipping away on our beer.

The following morning the news reporters came to see me and wanted to say in the paper that I was a hero. I asked them to not make me out to be that. I told them I just did what I needed to do to survive and save my friends, and didn't think of myself as being any kind of hero.

Sometime later, an investigation was made into the accident and a report made. I read it and it said that the water temperature was too cold for us to have been able to survive normally as the swim to shore distance was three miles in either direction. Also that we all would have drowned if we had not had the life jackets on.

There were over a hundred emergency calls reporting my boat fire and a few aeroplanes reported it as well, from as far away as White Island and the Blue Lake in Rotorua.

Towards the end of the fire my boat sank to the bottom of Lake Rotorua.

I really do believe that trusting God to help me do things so that they turn out OK, was very important and the right thing to do. God honours our faith in him.

Having faith can give us the ability to remain calm when others panic. It gives us you the ability to think things through and make the right choices – decisions that can mean the difference between life and death.

Praise the Lord! Glory be to God!

Walking through walls

This following story goes back to when I was 26.

I had been out to dinner with my partner Melanie, and a another couple called Carl and Sarah who were friends of mine from Auckland. We had a nice evening and after dinner Melanie and I headed home and went off to bed.

All seemed well and normal, however, in the middle of the night I woke up and saw a young man standing next to my bed looking down me. I yelled loudly at him and he departed quickly. The bizarre part is that he disappeared straight through the bedroom wall.

I was a bit shocked, as I thought at first I had a burglar in my house, but then I realized it was only a spirit. However, I got out of bed, walked out into the lounge, turned on the light and sat down on the couch.

A few moments later, several spirits walked through my lounge wall and stood in front of me. I could hardly believe my eyes – I could see them so clearly it was amazing. There were four of them, all teenagers, dressed in casual clothes – one of them was a girl.

Even though they appeared so clearly, I could tell that they were spirits, plus the clue was that they had just entered through the wall.

One young man had blond hair and he said to me, "We know you can hear us and we've come to you for help".

I asked him, "What kind of help do you want from me?"

He replied, "We're lost and don't know where to go or what to do."

I said, "OK. So what happened to you?"

The girl spoke and said that they had just been in a car accident. Somehow I did not feel afraid. I felt calm and decided I would try and help them.

I said that they needed to go into the light, and that would take them to heaven.

They asked how they were to do that. I answered that they should pray to God and Jesus, asking him to help them go where they needed to go. A few seconds later, a tunnel of bright white light appeared in my lounge room. It was like a tube of light about two metres (six feet) across, coming in from the roof to the floor. I encouraged them to walk into the light, then said that God was waiting for them to go now.

However, they hesitated and stepped back from the light. I urged them on, but they all continued to hesitate and two of them said they were afraid. So they just stood there looking at the light, and after about 15 seconds it just faded away and vanished, leaving the spirits still standing there.

I felt disappointed in them and couldn't understand why they did not take my advice. So I decided to take action and said very loudly, "In the name of Jesus Christ, be gone from here!" They all rapidly departed in different directions out of the walls, never to be seen by me again.

Melanie had stayed in bed until now, but she came into the lounge to see me and find out what was wrong after she heard me calling out to Jesus. So I told her what I had seen and what had happened. She spooked-out by it and stayed awake, cuddling up to me in bed until the morning.

However, for me, I learned that spirits are real and it confirmed to me that people have a spirit living inside of them. I have seen and spoken with a number of spirits since that night.

I had another similar experience when I was in my 30's. I was, standing in my kitchen talking to a friend, when over to my right I saw a woman step out of my refrigerator. Its door was closed at the time. She walked over to my friend and kissed him on the cheek then put her arm around his shoulder and looked at me and smiled.

So I began telling my friend about this woman, but as I was telling him, she faded away about 15 seconds after she first stepped out of the fridge. I told him that she was a beautiful young woman, with long brown hair and was wearing nice clothes, including a short skirt and knee-high boots. My friend didn't know what to make of it.

I had not been drinking and had not taken any drugs. It's just another experience I have had of seeing a spirit.

I hope that these stories will help open your eyes and your mind and get you thinking, and realise the truth and the realities of life.

May God be with us and may you find him now.

Do auras exist?

This experience happened when I was 24, while sitting in my car parked in the garage.

I had wanted to see a human aura for many years and I was thinking about it at the time. So I prayed for the ability to see an actual aura.

I was sitting in the driver's seat with my left hand on the manual gearshift, when, unexpectedly, I saw my arm radiating a bright blue. It completely surrounded my arm, extending out about 15 centimetres all around. It also appeared to have a purple tint to it.

In amazement, I just sat still, looking at what appeared, but it only lasted about 15 seconds and then vanished. I just stayed in the car pondering over what I had just seen. I was delighted and grateful that my prayer had been answered there and then, within seconds after my prayer and that I got to see this aura so clearly.

I decided to go and find someone to tell about what had just happened, so I got out of my car and went inside the house. My little brother Gabriel, who was only eight years old at the time, was sitting on the floor in the lounge occupying himself with something. I looked over at him and within two seconds, he was radiating blue light all around him. It radiated out from his head and all the way down his back a good 15 cm all around him. It seemed to be the same colour I saw around my arm – blue with a purple tint.

God only would know why we both were radiating the same colour aura that day. I must say it was an extraordinary experience and truly an amazingly wonderful sight to see.

The blessing for me was that I now know the human aura is a reality and that I know I have the ability to see them.

Praise the Lord!

Trips to Mount Ruapehu

I have done a little snow skiing, probably about twelve trips, to the snowy Mount Ruapehu.

I remember one night, after skiing on the mountain I was drinking in a bar with my friend Carl and I leant over the table to chat to a woman, as the music was very loud. Then I noticed a burning smell and flames began licking up around my face and head. It took me a few moments to pull my jumper up over my head and drop it to get the fire off me. Then a barman came and blasted the fire extinguisher at it.

I have another memory of getting a bus down the mountain. This bus was packed with people wanting to get down the mountain after a day's skiing. On the first corner it went too far to the left side of the road and the edge of the road gave way. The bus tipped over and slid on the snow for several metres.

We slowly managed to evacuate the bus one by one and I don't think anyone was hurt badly. I took a look after I had gotten free from the bus and saw that if it had kept sliding a few more metres we all would have gone over the edge of a long drop, to serious injury or death.

Up on the slopes I learnt to ski very quickly and seemed to be a bit of a natural at it. My friend Carl, an expert skier, liked me to tag along with him on the advanced ski trails. Double black diamond trails are the wildest and most dangerously adventurous.

I had quite a number of serious crashes on these trails and would hurtle down very steep slopes, sometimes flipping out of control and hoping for the best ending. I never hurt myself seriously snow skiing, but from time to time I would see the mountain staff taking someone down the mountain on a sledge stretcher.

My friend Carl was named 'Man of the Mountain' for two years running, taking the trophy for the fastest time down the mountain. He said I did very well at keeping up with him and following him down dangerous trails.

On another trip to the mountain I took my friend Greg along in my car and we were speeding along the road. We had sped up even faster to overtake a car and were doing about 160 kph (100mph) when I saw what looked like a car overtaking a big truck heading towards us.

I hit the brakes immediately and reduced speed as fast as I could, also using the manual gear box. But the truck and car zoomed closer, with the car still alongside the truck overtaking it.

I quickly realised I needed to give them more room, so I pulled my car over to the left, and with my car mostly off the road and just the right-hand side tyres on the edge of the road, WHOOSH, the truck and car went past us. We were still travelling at high speed at the moment of passing. Then I pulled my car back onto the road.

Much too close for comfort though. I have driven my car off the road a few times over the years to avoid a potential head-on crash like that.

Later that day Greg and I decided to go right to the top of the mountain, avoiding the crowds mid-way up the mountain. We got on the giant T-bar lift and up we went. At the highest point that the lift could take us up the mountain, there was a sign that said 'Extreme Skiers Only' and another sign next to it, saying 'Closed Due to Icy Conditions.'

We got off the lift and talked about this, but then discovered we had no other way to get back down the mountain except to ski down. The T-bar that took us up could not take us back on to down again. So even though we were not extreme skiers, we decided we would take on the challenge.

We counted to three and pushed off from the top. Away we went, zig zagging our turns on the slope in an effort to keep our speed under control. It was slippery on the ice and hard-out alright, but we did not fall over and had lots of fun, just laughing together and really buzzing.

Then we decided to head back up for another blast down the steep, slippery slope. We were the only ones crazy enough to not take notice of the warning signs.

On the lift we went, time and time again. Actually we crashed sometimes and slid at high speed, flipping down this steep slope, yet we did not care, nor did we get any pains worthy of mention. Just fabulous!

Tumbling from the sky

When I was 26 years old I decided to try sky-diving. The thought of it was a bit scary at first, but I wanted to do it anyway.

I really enjoyed my first tandem sky-dive and was eager to do it again, so I did two more. Then I was keen to take my girlfriend Melanie for one.

It wasn't the perfect day to choose for this next jump. There was a bit too much wind and the manager had to decide whether to cancel the jump or give it the go ahead. However, the instructor that I was to be strapped to was the same one who had taken me for my second sky-dive and he wanted to take me for a wilder ride this time. So we were given the go ahead and got into the plane and off down the runway and climbed to 9,000 feet.

Then we got ready to jump, sitting on the edge of the doorway. Out we went, into a tumble roll and then rotating around. My instructor headed into a dive called a staple dive, and we rocketed off, pointing straight down. My face and mouth were flapping as you do speeds of 300km per hour in a staple dive.

Then my instructor tried to flatten us out to slow us down, but we hit wind turbulence and went into flipping around and around, again and again. I could see my instructor moving his arms in different directions to stabilise us and I tried to do the same, but we just kept flipping over and over. One second I would see the ground, then the sky, then the ground again. I thought, "I don't think we're going to pull out of this in time. We're going to crash into the ground and die." I pleaded, "Please God, please God, I don't want to die."

This may have helped, as we started to slow down and were not flipping as fast. My thought was that now was the time to pull the parachute open. Relieved I heard the rustling sound of it opening. However it was a very abrupt opening that was hard on my neck as there was a brutal jolt due to the speed we were falling at.

He asked me if I was OK and I answered, "Yes, I'm good now the chute is open." He then told me we were coming in to land and to adjust my leg straps ready to come in and land on my bottom. I said "No, I want to land on my feet this time."

We landed well and on our feet. People clapped in relief, as while we were falling, those watching, including the manager of the skydive business thought for sure we were going to die. I was elated I was alive but if we hadn't pulled the chute open when we did we would have slammed into the ground just seconds later.

Thank you Lord!

Freak waves

I was out for a day trip on my 18-foot Barracuda boat named Kalua, with my Dad, younger brother Gabriel and his friend. I was 27 at the time.

We got off to a rough start as we were crossing the notorious Whakatane River bar. I went a little too fast into one of the waves and we launched up and over the wave that was crashing down hard and with the boat on an angle. The boys got knocked around the most, and we all had to climb up off the floor of the boat and get back up on the seats. A few bruises, but my crew were still keen to continue as it was a lovely day.

We headed over to the Rowe Rimu Islands. The day before I had put out a couple of crayfish pots and wanted to check them. We arrived and the water was calm apart from a rolling two-metre swell that seemed nothing to worry about.

Dad and I were pulling up one of the cray pots when I glanced out to sea and noticed something strange – the horizon looked different. It was as if there was a huge wave coming, but a long way out from us. I sensed something was seriously wrong, even though it was hard to see if it was really a wave or not.

I pulled the life-jackets out and told my crew to put them on. They did not want to as it didn't seem rough enough to need a jacket. I demanded that they put them on. The boat motor had stopped while we were pulling up the cray pot too, so I needed to restart the engine. It was an old 115hp Mercury outboard and very temperamental. I did not put my own jacket on yet as I felt the most important thing to do was to get the engine running. It's essential to be under power and drive into a big sea to survive.

I turned the ignition but the motor wouldn't start. I tried again and again. I looked out to sea and saw that I was right, there was a big wave on its way.

I thought, "Shit, we're about to get taken out by a tsunami."

I put my life jacket on and again tried to start the engine but again it wouldn't fire up. This wave was now getting too close for comfort. It was now more than ever apparent to me that if the engine was flooded, it was not going to start and we could all end up dead.

I prayed earnestly and then tried the engine one more time, and thank goodness it burst into life. I gave it a good revving then popped it into gear. I headed the nose of the boat into the oncoming wave and cruised at about 10 knots. Looking over to the left I saw the wave smashing into the island and going right over the top of it.

This wave was about 30 feet high and it was about to hit us. I kept the boat steady and in came the wave and up it we went. Up and up then over the top. It was unbelievable that in a relatively calm sea we got hit by a 30-foot wave. Then looking ahead, I could see another wave, just as big coming in on us. We braced ourselves and up and up and over we went again. It was awesome to ride up and over them. Then another was coming at us, then another. I counted five of them, but the last two were not as big as the first ones, yet still a challenge.

Thank God the engine started and we were able to power into and over them. Otherwise we would have been picked up, rolled, and dumped into the sea and our boat sunk. Not to mention trying to survive 30 foot waves in lifejackets designed for sheltered waters.

On the TV news that night they said that here had been volcanic activity at White Island and under the sea along the fault line, causing underwater eruptions. So they were just freak waves, generated from volcanic activity. If it had been a genuine tsunami there would have been a huge wall of water pushing up behind the wave, which would have gone in-shore over the land a long way.

It still seemed like a tsunami to us though. Beware of freak waves – they can catch you unawares and wipe you out.

Nearly beached

There we were, on another day that same year, my partner Melanie and I parked next to the Whakatane River bar, trying to decide if it was too rough to go fishing, or to go anyway and see what would happen.

Melanie had her heart set on going fishing, so I decided we would put the boat in the water, again my 18-foot Barracuda. We put our life-jackets on and headed for the mouth of the river bar. It was a wild ride – we smashed our way through the heavy waves then cruised through the big swells.

We decided on a spot to do some fishing, then put out the anchor and dropped our lines in. It was not long before I got a good bite and a hook up. I started to reel in the fish but lost it. I discovered it had bitten through the line. I suspected it was a barracuda as they have razor-sharp teeth.

I had a steel trace so put it on and tried again. Not long after, I got another hook up and it felt like a decent sized fish. I got it up to the boat and scooped it out with the net. To my surprise it was a shark, a hammerhead , about three feet long. Well, Melanie went ballistic – she screamed and jumped up on the seat, lifting her feet high in the air away from the shark's teeth. She made me kill it and secure it well away from her before she would even put her feet back down in the boat.

I put fresh bait on and dropped my line again. Minutes later I had another hook up and it was an even bigger fish this time. I played it for a while until it got tired out. I got it up to the side of the boat and it was another hammerhead shark, this time four and a half feet long. I got Melanie to hold my rod while I scooped the shark up in my net and finally managed to get it into the boat. It was flapping around and Melanie was screaming again with her feet in the air. It took me quite a while to sort this large fish out. After killing it and stowing it away, Melanie put her feet back down in the boat. I made sure it was well away from her as sharks can bite even though they're dead – it's their nerves still firing. It was now heading for my freezer and would make a few tasty meals.

Then I decided it was time to head home but would troll a lure on the way. I was hoping to catch a kingfish. We got a few hundred metres off the bar when I got a hook up and WOW it was a good size. My reel was whizzing as the fish pulled out the line. I put the boat in neutral and grabbed my rod from the holder. This fish put up a good fight – I would play it and reel it close to the boat and then it would panic and rip the line out from my reel.

This went on for quite a while, and then I noticed that we were dangerously close to the beach and the big three metre swells were going to dump and roll us onto the beach. I stuck my rod into the rod holder, then got in the skipper's seat to turn the engine over. It did not start first pop – it had stopped again while I was playing the fish.

I tried it again, and then again. If it didn't start immediately there would be no hope for us. Then finally it burst into life. I was so relieved. I put it in gear and opened it up. Half a minute longer and we would have been dumped onto the beach. We powered up the waves and over them, heading out into deeper water. Melanie wasn't aware how close we had come to disaster – not only was it dangerous, but it would have been a mission to recover the boat had we been beached.

After we had gone some distance off shore, I grabbed my rod and found that the fish was still on my line, so I worked away at the reel and focused on my fight with the fish. It took some time but I got it up to the boat and discovered it was a nice big kingfish. I was very pleased but it wasn't in the boat yet and I didn't want this one getting away. Melanie tried scooping it out of the water a few times, but it was a lot bigger than the net. Then I gave her the rod and told her to keep the line tight and I scooped the kingi up and out of the water – half the fish in the net and half hanging out. It was only a 15 kg (33lb) Kingi but was my biggest one so far.

We headed for the bar and had a wild ride in and across it. The shark and the kingi tasted great and we had plenty to put into the freezer as well.

I believe that if you have a lot of faith, God has your back, and he honours you and helps out.

What a trip. Glory be to God. Amen!

Saving the day

This story took place when I was 28. My friend Bill and I and his son Chad and my brother Gabriel, had all gone down to the East Coast for a weekend away. Bill and I planned to do some diving off the rocks.

The East Coast is about a five hour drive from Rotorua, and we were going to stay with friends of Bill. We unpacked our dive gear and then set off in the car to find a dive spot.

As I drove along the coast, Bill spotted an area that he wanted to dive from. So we put on our wet suits, tanks, and gear and entered the water from the rocks. The water was a little cloudy but not too bad. We bagged a feed of crays and made our way out of the water and across the rocks back to the car.

It was about a 20-minute drive back to the place we were staying. All was going well until we came up behind a truck. As it was going down a long hill I looked past it, and even though the road did have some bad bends in it, I had a clear view and decided it was safe to pass.

My passing the truck started off OK, but as the truck came to the next corner it did not stay on its side of the road, instead it used the whole road, including our lane, pushing us completely off the road while we were travelling at about 115km (70mph) per hour.

Suddenly we were sideways on gravel and dirt, heading for a large tree. I thought if I don't pull us out of this, we're going to die. I put my foot hard on the gas and the front tyres spun on the gravel. I backed the gas off a little as the tyres spun too fast, but leaving them spinning, I got them up onto the edge of the tarseal road and planted my foot hard. As the car clawed its way back up on to the road, I adjusted the steering wheel and we straightened up with a bit of a fish tail. I looked in the rear vision mirror and saw loads of tyre smoke from behind. My heart was beating fast and I was so grateful I had avoided us smashing into the tree side-ways.

59

We decided to chase the truck and have words with the driver. So I sped up and caught him, giving him signals to pull over. As it turned out, Bill knew the man and he rode in the hunt club with us. He was apologetic for not looking in his mirror before using up the whole road on the corner.

Anyway our weekend had turned out fine and we got home safe and sound.

Trust in God and he will give you the courage and guidance to take you to safety. Amen.

Whakatane bar

A year later and I'm 28. It's Christmas time and I'm staying at my friend Bill's batch in Ohope.

It just so happens that my friend Carl and his wife Sarah have come down from Auckland and are staying at a camping ground just down the road from us.

Bill and I are going to take the boat out and go for a dive. I invite Carl and Sarah to come along and they are delighted. We head over the hill to Whakatane with Bill's 18-foot boat named The Warrior.

After putting the boat in the water we put life-jackets on for the often dangerous Whakatane River bar crossing. However the weather and sea report was fine so we had no problem crossing it and got over the incoming waves nicely. We then headed for Whale Island, six miles away. It was a bit lumpy and bumpy on the way but not too bad.

After arriving safely I chose a spot to go for a dive. Bill said he did not want to dive today as he was not in the mood, therefore I decided to go on my own. I put on my wet-suit and swim gear. We did not put the anchor out as the water was too deep. Bill was to leave the engine running while I went for my dive.

Over the side I went and made my descent. On my way down I saw thousands of little jellyfish in the water. I got down to 25 metres, about 85 feet, and looked for crayfish but did not have any luck. I really wanted to take some crays home for my friends so kept searching and eventually came across some in behind some rocks in a small cave. It was a tight fit to get to them and I needed to go in a little further to reach them. I got hold of one and put it in my dive bag, but the crays then moved back further and were now out of reach, so I decided to back out of the cave.

However I got stuck and had terrible trouble getting free. It took over one agonisingly long minute. It's not good to dive alone. I checked my dive gauge and saw I was on the red line and needed to ascend right away. Thank goodness I was not stuck any longer than I was. My BCD (Buoyancy Control Device) was an integrated weight vest and held two pouches of lead weights and unbeknown to me. I had lost one of them trying to get out of the cave. My gauge was also indicating my nitrogen blood level was high, so a slow ascent was imperative.

I started to ascend, and on my way up dumped some air out of my air compensator and buoyancy regulator (BCD) but this did not slow me down, so I knew something was wrong. I dumped more air but I was still rising too fast. I grabbed at my weights and finding half of them gone, realised what had happened.

So I flipped upside down so my head faced down, and my fins upwards, and flipped them rapidly. I made sure I kept breathing and did not hold my breath – it is a death trap to hold your breath on the way up.

I reached for my emergency dump valve positioned at the rear and base of my BCD, but could not find it either. I was now in an out of control ascent and knew it could spell disaster. I kept trying to find the dump valve as I was heading to the surface but just couldn't.

I popped up at the surface close to the boat, pulled my regulator out of my mouth, and gasped, "Shit, I came up too fast, I think I've got the bends."

I swam to the boat, climbed on board and got out of my dive gear. I then called the Coastguard on VHF radio and informed them I might have the bends and could therefore need a helicopter to fly me to Auckland for decompression. The bends can kill you – or can leave you paralysed for life, also, if you hold your breath on the way up, the air expands and splits your lungs apart, killing you.

The Coastguard told me to wait and see if I get pain in my joints before they call the helicopter. They also informed us of a rise in wind speed that had made the bar unsafe to cross, so it was closed and we should stay at Whale Island until further notice. The bar had 3 to 4 metre (10 to 12 foot) waves crashing on it.

We found a sheltered spot and put the anchor out. Carl and Sarah did some fishing. When we explained to Sarah the sea and bar conditions she burst out in tears – she was not a happy camper. After a time, Bill got tired of waiting and wanted me to take us home. Even though the bar was closed he did not care, as he had faith in me being able to get us home safely. We attempted to lift the anchor but could not, it was stuck fast. After several attempts we gave up and tied the anchor rope to a buoy and left it behind. I handed Sarah a life-jacket and she burst out in tears again. Her husband Carl did his best to console her.

It was going to be a wild ride home and the bar conditions would be extremely dangerous. On the way home the sea was coming at us on the port side (left side) of the boat. This makes it tricky and dangerous in a big sea. As we got closer to the bar the VHF radio came on, warning us to turn around and not to attempt to cross the bar.

We ignored this and kept heading for it. They were warning us of four meter (12 foot) waves on the bar. I did my usual thing, followed a wave into the bar and riding over it just after it crashed. That went fine, but then we were suddenly hit by a large wave that spun us sideways. This was extremely dangerous and I acted immediately, turning the wheel to the left, then giving it the gas.

The propeller cavitated, not gripping in the water, so I backed off the throttle then re-applied the power. As the boat started to straighten up the nose lifted up high and I could not see. I had to do everything by feel. I backed off the gas when the boat was straight, then straightened the wheel, and thank goodness the bow started coming down.

I gave it the gas and powered over the bar, bouncing our way through, with rocks on either side of us. There was no room for any mistakes. The coastguard officer came on the radio and congratulated us for a spectacular crossing. While we were putting the boat on the trailer, the coastguard came down to the ramp to meet us and shake my hand.

In the end I had only a mild dose of the bends, with sore knees and joints, so did not request the rescue helicopter. What a day that was, with several things potentially fatal.

I firmly believe that having a lot of faith allows you to remain calm and work your way through danger with a sense of peace and a knowledge that God is helping.

The wild ocean

One fine day, my friend Bill, his son Chad and I decided to go to White Island for a dive trip. We again went in Bill's 18 foot boat The Warrior again. White Island is about 30 miles from Whakatane – we had a full tank of gas and the water was calm.

When we got about half-way to White Island the sea became a little rough, but not a concern. We came across a pod of dolphins following our boat. They were swimming along in front of us at the bow. It is always a pleasure to me to see the dolphins join in racing along with the boat.

We decided to stop and Chad and I jumped overboard with a mask and snorkel, hoping to swim with the dolphins. However, they soon scattered and disappeared, so I suggested to Chad we get out of the water as it was possible a shark might be around.

We arrived later at White Island, which is renown for being volcanic. Then Bill suggested we cruise over to a another small island not too far distant, and dive. He said it was an old dumping ground from the Second World War and that we might find some old artillery shells to take home.

I replied, "That sounds good, but I'm a bit concerned about the fuel – we want to make sure we preserve our supply".

But Bill was adamant he wanted to dive at the old dumping site, so I gave in and we set off for the small island. When we got there we suited up in our wet suits and dive gear and plunged into the water. At about 20 feet deep there was the top of a ledge that dropped off in a steep slope. We descended in our hunt for military shells. The slope was made up of boulders and I went inside the cracks between the boulders looking for shells.

I couldn't find any though, and noticed that my depth gauge was reading about 28 metres, which is close to the maximum recommended recreational diving depth of 30 metres. As my air was getting low, I decided I would return to the top. I did not know where my dive buddy was, but that's not unusual for Bill, he often took off on his own when we would go diving.

I swam out of the crevice and started to swim for the top when suddenly I was hit by a downward current, pulling me down deeper. I was flipping my fins trying to go up, but to no effect. So I blasted air from my tank into my buoyancy vest to its maximum and thrust hard with my fins for propulsion. This to my relief worked and I managed at last to ascend upwards. But I was worried, before I corrected my descent, my depth gauge had shown a reading of 40 metres which may have been too deep for safety. Divers often black-out unconscious at 50 metres to the point of no return. That's a constant reminder to stay aware of what you're doing while diving and being careful.

Well we both got safely back to the boat and then headed back to White Island. It was a lovely, fine day as we were on the lea side of the Island, the calm side, sheltered from the wind.

But the day was not yet over.

More diving adventure

Back at White Island we went for our second dive of the day. Even though the nitrogen levels in my blood were up a bit, I was keen to go on my second dive. I soon lost Bill again, he had darted off as usual on his own adventure.

I found myself going deeper and deeper in search of crayfish. I was on a slope that just kept dropping off deeper and deeper. I did find a ledge and was hopeful for a bag of crays. Rather, it was full of moray eels that all stood up at my arrival and seemed to be laughing loudly at me. There was even a fish called a pink maomao and it seemed to speak to me.

I looked at my gauge and I was at 35 metres, 5 metres below the safety limit, and my nitrogen blood level was high. My gauge was a high tech one that estimated the nitrogen levels in my blood and even showed how long I could stay at a certain depth. Well the eels kept laughing at me and I knew I must ascend quickly to a shallower depth as I was 'narked', also called 'nitrogen narcosis'. But at the same time I felt a desire to take the regulator out of my mouth and swim off even deeper, which would result in certain death. I felt I was a fish and could breathe underwater.

However, I pulled my mind together and said a prayer and began to make my way up slowly, trying not to go over the recommended speed. I saw my gauge flash at me a few times, indicating I was ascending too fast. However I just let air out of my BCD to compensate and help slow my ascent. I sure did not want the bends.

As I ascended, my mind became more rational, and was no longer narked. However, I was also caught up in a current and it was sweeping me away. When I reached the top and broke the surface, I was on the last few moments of air supply and I had been swept about 200 metres away from the boat. It would be a real battle to swim against the current to get to it. As I got half way back I could see my dive buddy looking out the other side of the boat for me in the wrong direction, so I knew I wasn't going to be picked up by the boat. It was a real slog to swim back, but I finally made it.

Back at the boat, Bill explained that he kept looking out the other side of the boat because he thought the current was heading that way. Whatever, I was just pleased that I was still alive and to have faith that God was with me. This belief always brings a sense of calmness over me, even when in a dangerous and serious situation.

I love God and trust him to help me through danger and daily situations that arise, whether big or small.

Well anyway, this story does not end here.

And more...

Bill and Chad decided on doing some fishing, and we caught a couple, and then they wanted to stay out the night. However, I recommended that we head home now as the weather warnings were forecasting high winds and rough seas. But Bill was adamant that he wanted to stay at White Island overnight and that the weather would blow over and things would be fine. Well, it was his boat, so I let him call the shots.

However, I thought, and also said to Bill, that he often put too much faith in me with his decision making while we were boating as he was over-confident in my ability to skipper and drive the boat in dangerous conditions. In the previous story, I had already driven the boat in and across the dangerous Whakatane Bar crossing in extremely dangerous conditions when even the Coastguard was calling over the radio that we need to abort. But Bill was impatient and over-confident in my abilities – too much so for my comfort.

So we stayed out that night. But I was awaken during the night by Bill telling me the anchor had broken free and the sea had gotten rough as the wind had changed direction. We had trouble holding anchor all night and used more gas than we would have otherwise, due to this problem. It was a long night and we had to stay awake for safety's sake.

In the morning the wind had shifted again and things seemed calm again, but I warned Bill that the sea around the corner of the Island would be rough and the way home was going to be rough.

I did not know at that stage how bad the sea was going to be. I called the coastguard, asking for a weather and sea conditions report, and they reported back that the wind was high and coming off shore from Whakatane, and the sea would have 6 metre (19 foot) swells offshore. I wasn't happy – we only had an 18 foot boat on a sea that was massive.

I then thought of a tourist boat that came out to the island regularly, named PJ. It's a 60-foot boat and I thought I would try and reach them on the VHF radio. They replied and happened to be parked up just around the corner from us, waiting for the conditions to improve. So I made an arrangement to follow them back to Whakatane when they were ready to leave.

An hour later, they called us on the radio and said they were about to get underway, and soon after we saw them come around the corner of the island and pulled in behind them ready for our trip home. We had our life-jackets on, but they were rated only as 'sheltered water life-jackets' – not exactly ideal for 6 metre swells. We would still be in danger of drowning if we ended up in the water.

As we rounded the side of the island exposed to the wind, Bill and Chad were scared just looking at the massive waves. I prayed for safety, strength and guidance and thought of the strong faith I always relied upon, and away we went.

It was indeed hard-going and the guys were terrified. Bill crouched down in the front of the cabin as he couldn't cope with it. PJ was up ahead but travelling too fast for us. We were doing 28 to 32 miles per hour and PJ just kept getting further ahead of us. I was not scared, but I was concerned. We were doing really well at one stage as PJ must have slowed down a little, letting us gain ground. We could see lots of tourists on PJ looking back at us and some waving. Then PJ seemed to get away from us again.

We were flying along really well though, when suddenly we got hit somehow by a wave and swamped. The boat was suddenly bogged down with water and I looked back and it was not a good sight – we had taken on a lot of water. We felt vulnerable and again got hit by another wave. I flicked the switch for the bilge pump, but it was slow to pump water out of the boat. I managed to get it moving again but it was slow to get up to speed properly – only half of what we were doing before. PJ now seemed to be miles away at this stage and we were in danger of being swamped again and sinking.

We were really getting bashed around badly by the sea. However, the bilge pump kept pumping and the water in the boat slowly lessened and we gained more speed. We had to

70

bash through about 20 miles of 6 metre waves, but then they got smaller and smaller over the next 10 miles, as the wind was coming off-shore.

Looking back, I think that we most likely would have drowned if we had sunk in those 6 metre waves. But we didn't, and yet again survived to tell the tale. We got to little 1 metre waves, and then suddenly the engine conked out, as we were out of gas. The extra effort the engine had to perform in the very rough conditions used up any surplus fuel. Luckily, a nearby boat named Moby Dick, responded to our radio call and gave us a tow back home the last 3 miles.

So we got home safely and have some good memories from that trip, except that Bill was so traumatised from the excursion that he promptly sold his boat.

Just another exciting adventure I thought I would share, and one of several where I had faith that God would get me home safely.

The Great White shark

It was a fine winter's day for scuba diving at Motiti Island, 16 miles off the coast of Tauranga in the Bay of Plenty, New Zealand. So I went for a scuba dive with a friend of mine named Glen. We had headed out to the island on his father's launch. I was 29 at the time and I enjoyed scuba diving in winter as the visibility was good underwater and you could see well into the distance.

All was going well, but I could not find any crayfish. I looked over to see how my dive buddy was doing and saw that his scuba tank was floating above his head and he was holding his regulator in his mouth. So I swam over to help him and pulled the tank down and started to strap it back in place on his back.

We were on the ocean floor at a depth of 12 metres or 40 feet. Just as I was trying to fasten his tank back in place, he started thrashing around and pointing at something. However, I thought I must fasten his tank in place before anything else. Just as I secured the strap for his tank, he accidentally knocked my dive goggles off my face, and they fell to the sea floor. I could hardly see a thing, just a glimpse of green on the sandy sea floor. I reached down and searched around by feel, found them and put them back on. I proceeded to blow the water out of them to clear my mask, as the water level was going down in my mask.

Then I saw my dive buddy pointing again. I looked over in that direction and a long way away I could see what at first glance appeared to be a whale. Then I thought, "Its tail is going slowly from side-to-side, so it can't be a whale. Whale's tails go up and down. This is like National Geographic. I need a camera." Then I concluded that it must be a shark, and a massive one at that. I knew it was wise to follow the golden rule of scuba diving, 'DO NOT PANIC, REMAIN CALM'.

My dive buddy swam off and I chose not to follow him but to remain still and not attract the shark's attention. I also did not want to swim to the surface as that's a very dangerous thing to do when a shark is present. I could see it was getting closer and that it was a massive one. I could also see its mouth was partly open and could also tell that it was the king of all sharks – the Great White.

My heart was racing and it was swimming directly for me but I chose to remain still and stay put, so as to not directly attract its attention. I pulled my dive knife out from my leg pouch and thought I will fight for my life if need be, and it's looking that way. It was a female Great White as only females can grow to this awesome size.

I prayed to God and Jesus to help me to survive, and thought of how I must have faith that I will be OK, that I am in God's hands and will survive this ordeal. I also promised not to sin any more if God saved me. So I stayed put on my knees on the sandy sea floor.

The shark was swimming slowly, but directly for me and I thought I was about to be eaten alive and what a horrible way that was to die. It was almost as if I could hear the sounds on the Jaws movie as it was approaching me. As it got to about 12 feet away from me, two big kingfish swam very quickly between the shark and myself as if they were swimming for their lives. And with that the shark turned a 90 degree angle and followed them.

At that moment I had a nasty thump in my chest and a lot of pain – it felt like my heart had stopped beating altogether. Then about three seconds later it started pumping again, but I was still in a lot of pain. I thought, "O my God, not only was I in terrible danger of being eaten alive, but now I'm having a heart attack and may die from that anyway."

I just stayed put, crumpled over on my hands and knees, and watched the shark swim after the kingfish. I was totally amazed at the size of this shark as it looked to be over 20 feet in length and the size of its tail and dorsal fin was something to behold.

Then I watched as it circled around underneath some fish that were swimming on the surface. It headed up to the top at high speed and launched half way out of the water. Its body crashed back into the water and I saw it chomp twice and its gills flap, then a large fish tail falling from the surface to the sea floor, and a thought horrified me, "That could have been me!"

I then went looking for my dive buddy but could not see him, but I did see a rock ledge and decided to get under it for some protection. I did not want to go to the surface yet as it's a very dangerous place to be with a large shark present. As I snuggled into the ledge I realised that my breathing was too rapid and I needed to slow it down and conserve the air in my tank.

After a few minutes I noticed my air gauge was in the red zone, telling me it was time to get going. Just as I started to depart from the ledge, my dive buddy appeared in front of me and made a signal to head to the top. We swam along the bottom until we were under the boat, then made our way to the top. I could not see where the shark was, which I was not happy about – sharks love attacking people from underneath.

Just as I was about to get out of the water from the boat ladder, my dive buddy kicked me, making me fall back in the water. He was panicking and wanted to get out of the water first. I remember waiting and being very worried, as I did not want to be bitten in half.

Finally, I got back on the boat, and taking my dive gear off was a wonderful feeling, having survived and cheated death once again.

We lifted anchor and went further along the island a mile or so, and then decided to brave it and go for a second dive. So, over the side we both went.

I made my way over to the rocks in about 20 feet of water and started inspecting holes to find crays. I looked into one hole, thinking that it looked like a perfect spot for a cray, when suddenly a massive conger eel jumped out at me with its jaws wide open. It was right in my face and looked as if it would have been able to bite my head off, it was so big. That was enough for me for the day. I made my way back to the boat and wanted to get out of the water as I was worried the shark would make its way over and find me.

I feel God did answer my prayer that day, and possibly made the two kingfish swim between the shark and myself, thus distracting it away from me, and my failing heart seemed to come right.

In the midst of all this, I had faith that God would help me and that things would be OK. This is what helps in keeping me calm and brings a strange sense of peace when I think panic and fear would take over. God knows when you have faith and believe and honours that and helps you.

Praise the Lord I say!

Who's shooting at me?

This next experience I had when I was 29 and had gone scuba-diving down the East Coast of the North Island with my friend Bill.

It took about six hours for us to get there, towing the boat. Bill and I went down for a dive and sometime during the dive we lost each other, so I came back to the boat a bit early, although I still had air in my tank.

I had taken my dive gear off and was standing on the boat when I heard a whirling sound coming towards me and wondered what it was. Then I heard a crack followed by a loud bang and a rolling sound like thunder. I thought, "That can't be thunder, it's a sunny fine day. That must be a rifle and it must be shooting at me – my goodness, this is not good at all."

So I ducked down in the boat where the shooter would not be able to directly see me. I remember thinking about how I had heard that when someone shoots at you, the bullet passes or hits you before you hear the sound of the gun going off.

I thought, "I'm definitely being shot at here." I felt vulnerable because I was about 150 metres (155 yards) off-shore in a boat and the shot came from the shore direction. "How will I be able to drive the boat back to shore while being shot at?" I thought. I prayed and asked for courage and protection from this shooter.

My dive buddy arrived back at the stern of the boat and I got up and went over to help him into it. I said, "Bill, someone just shot at me." He did not believe me at first but then he changed his mind, and I got him to get into the bow cabin up the front of the boat where he would be safe. I remembered my Uncle Ray who had served six years in Vietnam as an officer and wondered, "What would he do right now?"

I decided to hope for the best and went up to the bow and pulled the anchor up. So far so good it seemed, so I decided I would stand up in the boat and drive it into shore. And in we went. I did some zigzags so that we weren't going in a straight line, making it harder for any shooter.

It was a stressful ride into shore as it appeared that we would still be in danger while loading the boat onto the trailer. Although I did not hear the rifle go off again, I knew it had to be a large calibre one, due to the loud sound it made.

Once on the shoreline, I got out of the boat and looked along the bushes on the hillside, to see if I could spot the sniper, but couldn't. Then we just got on with loading the boat onto the trailer and got out of there quickly. To do this we had to drive up a winding road, up a hill surrounded in bush and I was not at ease until we had made it onto the main road.

When I was back home in Rotorua, the police told me there had been another incident of a man shooting at people who were crayfish diving down that way. I told the police I was not happy with them, as when I was on the boat and had rung them, I was just put through to the local police station at Te Kaha. And all they did was tell me to come into the police station and file a written complaint. So even though I had explained that I was out in my boat being shot at right then, the police would not come out to see if they could find the shooter. Honestly!

However, I was happy to be alive, and I feel that God gave me courage and a sense of peace that helped me to make it home safely that day.

More target practice?

Ten years later, someone else tried to shoot me. A lady friend I loved dearly had come to stay with me for the weekend. Although we had been friends for six years, I had not seen her for three months. She did not want a romantic relationship and just wanted us to be friends. Her name is Diane and she is a lovely red head.

Late one evening we were in my bedroom watching TV, when I heard a car pull up outside, and the sound of voices. After awhile, when there was no knock at the door, I took a look.

The car was parked in front of my steps and a man was standing out there in the open. I heard him say, "It's definitely her's." Diane's car was also parked out front and he was standing next to it.

Another man noticed me and said, "There's a guy, jump in the car," then they drove off down the driveway.

I thought this was a bit odd and went and asked Diane if she had been seeing another man in the last three months? She said she had not been. However, by what the man had said, I was not convinced and suspected she might be lying to me.

About an hour later, when lying in bed, I saw through my bedroom door the beam of a flashlight up on the lounge room wall. The light in the lounge was off, so the beam of the flashlight was easy to see. It was moving so I knew someone must be standing outside the house, holding a torch. I got out of bed and carefully looked out the bedroom door, just poking my head around the corner.

The outside light was on and the curtains were pulled, so I could see the glass door and I saw two men standing at my door. One of them was holding something long and I wondered if it was a rifle.

Then one of them said, "There he is, shine the light up on the door frame."

Then I heard him say, "Quick, do it now." I saw the one holding the long thing lift it up. I pulled my head back behind the door frame and ducked down.

Then I heard him say, "F**k, the gun's jammed. Hurry, let's get out of here before he calls the police."

Then I heard footsteps down the stairs. I was pretty concerned that someone had just made an attempt to shoot me. I did not ring the police as I thought that they would be long gone before the police arrived.

Diane still maintained that she hadn't been seeing a man. I felt that she had been, and he'd become jealous at her spending the weekend at my house, so wanted to shoot and kill me.

I did ring the police the next day, but in my eyes they were hopeless. They spoke with Diane and just took her word for it and did no further investigations. They said there was nothing to go on. So I suggested they look into her phone records and they may discover the culprit. The police said that would be an invasion of Diane's privacy.

I replied disbelievingly, "So do I have to be actually shot dead on the floor for you to do a proper investigation. Come on now!"

Well anyway, as I see it, I'm still alive thanks to the grace of God. Halleluiah!

Last dive?

A few months later, I had another encounter with a couple of sharks. They were not as big as the Great White and I remained calm and survived that too. However, several months after this encounter I was diving and decided I was not happy with what I was doing. I was not enjoying my diving any more as it always seemed to include looking over my shoulder for sharks. So, while underwater I decided that this would be my last scuba dive.

I've had a lot of close encounters with death in my life, and for me, I choose to believe that my survival is more than luck and that God has been helping me survive, time after time. Although I was worried and concerned, I was overcome with a strange sense of peace and calmness during these experiences – even a sense of not fearing death. For example, even when thinking of the shark biting and ripping into me, there was still a sense of peace within me.

Two days after I saw the Great White, a helicopter pilot measured one against a boat and it was 18 foot 6 inches. I think this is most likely the same shark. The one I saw seemed over 20 feet long, but diving goggles can make fish under water look larger than they really are.

I know that some people have not believed this shark story, let alone believing some of my other stories. I have an understanding of and a compassion for how people doubt things and find it hard to believe the unusual, but for myself, I truly believe in many strange things, as I have experienced them personally.

There is a message in that. God bless you all!

Under a spell?

I was now 30 years old and it was May 2001. That was when my mental breakdown happened.

It began with an operation six months before. The surgeon had made a botch job of it and as a result I was suffering a lot of pain. I had bottled up resentment and anger for most of those six months since the operation. I had also been smoking some marijuana for a couple of months to help ease the pain, but had not had a drink for about two and a half years.

On a Friday morning, I woke up to the sound of footsteps outside my house, and looked out the window and saw a man walking off down my driveway. I got out of bed and went outside and found a piece of paper on the bonnet of my car. There was also a smooth rock, a small piece of bread, and what seemed to be two human hairs. On the paper was writing and the words were all written backwards and it seemed to be some kind of spell.

After reading it, I burnt it in the back garden and went back inside. Then I heard a large bird flying around above my house. It was squawking loudly, sounding like a crow. However, I could not see it when I went looking for it, I could only hear it. I was stressed out all that day at work. I had an idea about who had put the spell on my car bonnet, but couldn't prove it.

After work I rang my mother and she decided to come and visit me. She was concerned about this spell and how stressed I was about it. I felt that someone was messing with me and I was already at the end of my tether as it was, without this going on as well.

After we talked, she decided to ring my doctor, who put her onto the Mental Health Unit. This would be the first time I had anything to do with the mental health system.

I crack

Later I decided to drive to my friend Bill's farm, just out of town to tell him about this spell and to have a spa to help me relax. I grabbed and loaded my shotgun in case I was dealing with a serious situation and needing protection.

I went out and got into my car with the gun, and then noticed a man coming up my driveway as I was driving off, but did not stop and ask him what he wanted. As it turned out I should have, and things would then have turned out a lot better for me.

It was a man from the Mental Health Unit, and he had seen me getting into my car with the shotgun. However he did not ask my mother if I had a gun license, but instead immediately phoned the police, who deployed the Armed Defender's Squad.

Anyway, I arrived at Bill's farm and unloaded the shot gun and hid the shells. Then I went and had a spa pool and told my friend about this spell being laid on the bonnet of my car.

As Bill is a good friend of mine he was not happy about this spell either. He also felt it was OK that I had a gun with me for self-protection, if needs be.

Then the phone rang and kept on ringing, so I got out of the pool and answered it. It was my partner Melanie. She wanted me to come home but wouldn't tell me what for. She didn't tell me it was the police who were making her call me.

Well, I departed from Bill's place that night and drove down his long farm driveway. I had to stop to open the farm gate and thought, "What's going on here. This gate is always left open." I went on high alert as I sensed something was wrong.

Then all of a sudden, in the dark, I heard screeching, skidding tyres, then lights and sirens and police with rifles and spotlights were jumping out of a patrol car. I turned around and saw that the Armed Defenders were coming in from behind me. They must have been lying down in the grass waiting.

I started walking back to my car and police were yelling at me to get down on the ground. I looked down at my chest I could see bright red dots from the gun lasers. So I lay down on the gravel farm driveway as instructed. I couldn't understand why they were going about things this way, when all they had to do was walk up to me at the farm gate, and ask if they could speak with me, and all would have been fine.

The police went to my car looking for my gun. One of them spotted it, and another asked him if it was loaded. The other officer said, "Well if it's not loaded it will be in a minute."

I objected, saying "You can't do that. It would be framing me."

Another officer responded, "Shut up, we are above the law and can do whatever we like."

That angered me to respond, "You can't treat the public like that!." He replied in foul language and again said they could do whatever they liked. Well, I was now fuming and already at breaking point without any of this going on and I finally cracked.

I got up off the ground, even though the police were yelling at me to stay there. Then I quickly pushed that policeman's rifle out of the way and punched him in the nose. Then it was all on. I heard them yelling, "He is unarmed." Then police were coming at me. I punched and pushed a few of them. All I really wanted was to go home, but I was so angry that they ambushed me like that, when they should have just spoken to me. I would have told them what was going on and showed them my fire arms license. They handled things entirely the wrong way, and saying they were above the law was the last straw.

They were very aggressive and over the top with getting the handcuffs on me. They even kicked and pepper-sprayed me after they were on. The they deliberately tightened the handcuffs afterwards, cutting off my circulation, and would not loosen them. Later on, photos were taken in hospital as there was concern as to how I was handled. I was an utter mess.

Psychic experiences

As I lay there, face down and handcuffed on the gravel driveway, I experienced some very unusual phenomena, even for me. All of a sudden I started predicting things.

I said, "In four months to the day, two planes will crash into two high skyscrapers in New York and Bin Laden would be to blame. That 3500 people would die, including 300 firemen and 50 police officers.

I also looked up and saw numbers appear in the sky, they were in fluorescent blue. I said they were numbers for a big Wednesday lottery draw in five years time, with prizes of seven million and a silver Porsche car, which I saw in a clear and vivid vision. It was as if time was standing still, almost as if I had slipped into another realm.

Then I looked over and saw two men about 40 feet away and I called out for them to come over, which they did. They were dressed in dark blue overalls, with black boots, very much like the police, but with no badges on their clothing.

They lay down on the ground facing me, and one said, "It's OK Adrian, we are here to help." I could tell that they were spirits, not flesh and bone. Although they looked solid, somehow I could sense they were not human.

The one that did most of the talking had blond hair and blue eyes and looked about 40. He asked me what made me so psychic and said he could fix the problem of the tight handcuffs for me.

I refused his help, as I sensed he was an evil spirit even though he seemed nice. He offered me money and I declined the offer. He tried persistently to offer me money and said that no amount would be too much. He said he could sort the police out for me, and again I declined his offer. He would not tell me who he was and, when I began to pray, he definitely did not like it.

He suddenly turned nasty on me, pulling out a handgun and pointing it in my face and saying things that were nasty. I was not frightened at the time, but later on, for months fear would haunt me, as he was also threatening me with horrible things that would happen to me in the future.

Before he turned nasty, he asked me if I was ready to go ahead with the mission. I said yes, even though I did not know what he was on about. Then he said, "Good lad, but there is a chance you won't make it out alive. Do you still want to go ahead with the mission?" Again I said, "Yes." God only knows what he meant by that, but I did find out some things the hard way, over the next week ahead.

Before I go on, I want to say that, four months later the Bin Laden twin-tower attacks happened, and in the exact great detail as I had predicted. This was a huge shock to my system when I saw it on the TV and it made me worry that somehow I was responsible for the attack. It also left me in fear of what the spirit man had said regarding the nasty things that would happen to me.

Five years later I would witness the $7 million Big Wednesday draw happen, with the numbers I had predicted. Those Big Wednesday draws did not even exist at the time I made the prediction. I'll write more on this later.

Somehow I was charged up on supernatural powers and I even flashed my eyes, like a camera flashes, at this spirit man and at the police. Later I would find out I was having a breakdown mixed with psychosis. However, I believe things were not just in my mind and that these things can be more real than people think.

My conclusion as to who this blond spirit man was came to me while I was lying on the driveway – it surely had to be Satan himself or one of his henchmen.

More psychic scenes

Another highly interesting thing happened while I was lying face down on the driveway while the spirit of Satan and the police were there as well. I decided I wanted to remove my hand from the handcuffs. In my mind I believed I could do it, so I wriggled my wrist and removed my hand from the cuffs, however it was not as one thinks. I held my arm out in front of me but it was glowing and transparent. I could tell it was my spirit arm as my physical arm was still bound in handcuffs.

The policemen were amazed and one said, "That's very impressive," and another asked, "How do you do that?"

One of the officers wanted to shake my hand, so I lifted up my hand and shook his, and squeezed fairly hard. He couldn't believe that I had such strong physical strength and was amazed at this.

Another of the strange things was, it wasn't until the blond spirit and I had finished talking with each other that the police picked me up and carried me off to the police wagon. It was all extremely bizarre.

A further strange thing was, that it seemed the police were affected by the two demonic spirits. The way they were talking and dealing with me seemed to indicate this.

This was the first time I had ever been arrested. On my ride to the police station I got overwhelmingly hot, as never before, and it lasted for quite some time.

At the police station they had me sit and talk to a mental health worker named Eddie. He was taking down notes while the police gathered around and listened. They asked me questions as they seemed to believe I was psychic. This was because, back on the driveway earlier, I had told one officer his daughter's names and his correct cell phone number, and told other things to officers that made them believe I was psychic.

Well I am not psychic all the time, but when I have a clairvoyant moment, I can slip into a state of consciousness and predict in great detail, and this remains the case to the present day. The police also wrote down details I gave them in the police station regarding the future death of Sir Peter Blake. I will refer to this later.

In police custody

I was held in the Rotorua police station for several days, which turned out to be a nightmare. One time they came into the cell and beat me with a police baton and punched me. Another time I was worried they would kill me, as they would say unspeakable things to me.

On one occasion, I tried to escape custody while being transported from the court back to the station. An officer was threatening "To feed me to the dogs," so I head-butted him, unlocked the door and jumped from the moving police wagon. In the process I banged my head and broke my leg.

I was in the back seat, not the box on the back of the wagon. The officer sitting next to me stun-gunned me twice with a black Taser before I managed to leap off. Then they zapped me four more times with the Taser, even though I was just lying on the road with a broken leg. All up, they tasered me six times. It was like terror raining down upon me and I thought my heart was going to explode due to the amount of electricity running through my body. Unbelievable behaviour by the police I say.

I did not know if it was day or night in the cell, as a light was on continuously and the police would never tell me the time or the day.

Some days after my arrival at the cells (it seemed like a week ago) two officers came to tell me to come with them as they were taking me somewhere, but they would not say where. I had to walk backwards as my leg was broken and it was extremely painful to walk on. The police did not believe my claim that it was broken and ridiculed me for walking backwards. (Later, hospital x-rays confirmed a broken tibia and fibula. It was broken alright!)

They handcuffed me to the back seat of the police wagon and off we went. As we pulled out of the police station onto the road, suddenly the wagon started rocking from side-to-side and I heard moaning noises coming from the rear box section.

I asked the officers who was in the back and why there were these noises and motion.

They said, "Don't worry, it's normal." I thought, "Whatever it is, it can't be normal." I looked over my shoulder and peered through a little window into the box section of the wagon, and could just see what looked like a man with silver duct tape over his mouth. I couldn't believe this was happening and knew something was seriously wrong.

I could not understand what was going on. Was this the police playing a game with me to frighten me, or was this Satan himself playing with me to frighten me? Had God let Satan have go with testing me in this way, or was it the spell?

Things were out of my control and it felt like God was no longer there for me. So, was this a supernatural experience, and if so, was it a positive or negative one?

I did not know, but when I asked the police again why the van was swaying and the moaning was coming from the back, they said they were going to stop at a Hamilton park and they had a job for me there. I asked what this job was, and they repeated the same words, and added that it was to take care of the men that were in the back of the wagon. They also said they had what I would need to take care of these men.

Well, I could not believe what I was hearing and yelled, "No, no it's the spell, you must believe me, you are under the influence of a spell and Satan!"

Was this the police playing a game with me? Was it Satan, or was it Satan and the police? I repeated that and added, "You must let the men in the wagon go free. Do not harm them."

They replied, "We won't. It's you who is going to do that." At these words I knew I was in deep trouble, and my praying did not seem to be fixing the situation.

They pulled into the Hamilton park, about an hour's drive from the Rotorua police station. The officers said, "Well we're here, are you going to sort these men out?"

I was very concerned, and remembered then, that back while I was handcuffed on the farm driveway I had said, "Why all this drama? I've done nothing wrong, I'm just a little fish.

89

Why don't you go and arrest six of the worst criminals you can find and I'll take care of them." I was out of my mind when I had said this, and I was also face-to-face with the spirit I think was from Satan or was Satan himself.

It had now become clear to me that the police were trying to pin me for a more serious crime. I thought of how police read people their rights and say, "What you say or do may be held against you in court."

I said another prayer, then the police backed down and said surprisingly, "So you're not going to take care of these men then?"

I said, "No!" and they then started to pull away and back out onto the road again. I asked them to take me to hospital.

They said they could take me to hospital, or back to jail, but if they took me to hospital, I was not to say anything bad about the police, or leave any notes behind either. I agreed, so they in turn agreed to drop me off at the hospital.

However, they also threatened me if I said anything about the police. In addition, they got me to say that I was guilty into a small hand held tape recorder, even though they would not tell me what I was saying I was guilty for. I went along with it because I was in a lot of pain and really had to.

Inward struggles

They dropped me off at the Henry Bennett hospital in Hamilton, which I later found out was where psychiatric assessments are done.

They drove into the unloading bay and a roller door closed behind us. My handcuffs were removed and I called some male nurses over to help me walk. I told them I needed help as my leg was broken. These men came to assist me and I asked them, "Can you hear moaning coming from the wagon?" They said, "Yes".

I then asked them, "Can you see it rocking?" they said they could but assured me the police would not harm the men. I told the police I insist they let the men go free and that they must not harm them. I did the best I could at the time. I did not know exactly what was going on, but did know it was not good.

My arrival at hospital was a huge relief for me. The nurses were nice to me and I was just so relieved I had made it to safety. One male nurse told me they liked my style. I don't know why, but it was nice they said that.

However they also did not believe my leg was broken, so the following day I demanded an x-ray be taken of it. After they did so they apologised, saying it was indeed broken and arranged for me to have a cast put on it.

They would not give me crutches though, saying they could be taken off me by other men in the ward and used as weapons. This made it hard and painful to get around for a couple of weeks, so I had to get people to help me walk.

Speaking with psychiatrists was interesting. I told them about the arrest and the spirit of Satan, and that an angel had told me I must send a letter to the President of America and tell him of my prediction that Bin Laden was going to have jets fly into two skyscrapers.

Well, I was not allowed to send my letter, and found out later that they concluded I was experiencing a breakdown and a psychosis. I don't think those doctors realised that what I was experiencing was actually real, or a lot of what I experienced was real, and in another realm – the spirit realm.

Many doctors think that hearing voices is a part of the brain malfunctioning, and you are only hearing your own thoughts. That may be true in some cases, but I can assure you that the spirit world is highly complex. Many doctors also think that if we see a spirit walking around and talking with us, it is only an hallucination. I can assure you that in my experience this is not the case.

I was so fearful in the hospital, that one day I pulled a rubber sock the nurses had given me to put over the cast on my broken leg, over my head and tied my shoe lace around it and my neck. However when I could no longer breathe, I decided it was a horrible way to die and pulled the rubber sock off my head.

I know this whole set of experiences had a profound effect on me. I suffered mentally and emotionally for a long time afterwards, and had a lot of fear due to what the spirit man and police threatened would happen to me.

One thing led to another and this chain of events tipped my life upside down and over time I lost everything dear to me. I now believe Satan discerned my destiny with God and wanted to destroy it and my life as well.

I even lost hope and faith in God. I had decided sometime later, that God was no longer helping me so did not keep up my devotion or my spiritual journey. In other words, I gave up trying to please God and took my own road.

It turned out to be a long hard road for me. I call it my '15-Year Winter' and 'The Perfect Storm'. However, it did eventually bring me back to God, and I did stop drinking and smoking.

I basically had a 15 year struggle mentally, emotionally and financially. The time even came when I found myself living in a park for about two months and realised I had to make a drastic change in my life.

I began attending a church, which led to a member there inviting me to come and reside at a Christian rehabilitation centre called 'Stepping Stone Ministries'. There I managed to change and turn my life around and re-establish my relationship with God and Jesus, and I began to receive the Holy Spirit within me once again.

Hallelujah!

A near-death experience

While I was in the police cells in Rotorua, soon after being arrested, I had an experience I would now like to share. I think it was my second day in the cells. I was 30 years old at the time.

The police were not nice to me at all and I could not understand why. Surely they could see I was an unwell man. They should have been kind to me rather than the way they were behaving. I was not able to be strong and just brush off and ignore such behaviour towards me.

I felt my life was in danger and therefore said a prayer. While I was praying, I felt the Spirit of God enter me, totally consuming me with extreme intensity. It was totally overwhelming. I knew the feeling, as it was the third time in my life I had experienced this kind of extreme, intense connection with God. It was out of this world – in fact so intense that I felt as if I was part of God and God was part of me. Halleluiah!

It lasted a good 10 or 15 seconds then lifted, leaving me still with a nice, peaceful presence of the Holy Spirit.

I then prayed that I would become invisible to the police. Sometime later I heard the footsteps of a policeman coming down the corridor outside my cell and I prayed this again. Then there was the sound of the keys and the cell door opened and an officer stepped inside.

He said, "Adrian, where are you?" I looked at my arm and could see it, so thought I wasn't invisible, but the officer yelled, "Shit, where is he?"

Then, leaving the cell door wide open, he just walked off. I was amazed and thought, "Wow, it worked. He couldn't see me!"

So I walked out of the cell and down the corridor looking for a way out. Another policeman was walking towards me and I stepped to one side of the corridor and he just walked straight past me. Then I began to think, if I did escape, I would be on the run and the police would hunt me down. I pondered on this and then decided I did not want that, so I walked back to the police cell and sat down on the bed.

I prayed aloud and said, "I am visible again."

A few minutes later, several officers arrived at the cell and one said, "He is there! Is there something wrong with your eyes?"

Well, the first officer was adamant in trying to tell them that I was not in the cell when he checked on me.

The next day I asked if I could see someone from the mental health team. I'd been hearing voices off and on since my arrest on the driveway, but the real reason was that I felt my life was in danger and wanted to get the word out.

Sometime later I was told a man called Eddie from Mental Health was there to see me, and I was led from my cell down a corridor to another cell where he was waiting for me.

I said to him, "Eddie, I feel my life is in danger, and you need to get me out of here. If I die it will be the police that killed me."

I spoke quietly, as I knew a police officer was standing outside the door. However he must have heard me, as he said, "He's heard enough," and then walked away, returning about 30 seconds later with more officers. They said, "That's enough, you're coming with us." I said I hadn't finished yet and I needed to talk more to this man. I had talked to Eddie for less than a minute.

However, they just grabbed me – two officers held my legs, with one on each arm. Another held me in a headlock so tightly I struggled to breathe. As they carried me away and down the corridor I spluttered out, "I can't breathe!"

The officer responded by clamping down harder in his hold around my neck and completely cut of my air supply. I thought, "This is it, it's over. I'm going to die," and everything went black. It's a horrible feeling being choked to death.

The next thing I know, I'm speeding through a white tunnel for a few seconds. Then I find myself standing in a total white-out – it was like standing in a white cloud. I've sky dived through a white cloud so it was similar to a being in a cloud. I felt fine, great actually and I could see spirits walking around in the distance.

Then a female angel appeared – at least I assumed she was an angel, although she had no wings. But I remember that at the time, I felt like she was an angel.

She was beautiful and had long hair and a lovely sounding voice. She was standing right in front of me and said, "Adrian, you must go back now before it's too late, it's not your time yet."

I answered, "No, no, I'm not going back. I'm staying right here." I remember it felt good and also safe there, so I wanted to stay.

She repeated, "Adrian, you must go back now before it's too late, it's not your time yet".

Then she held up her hand and with the palm of her hand did a pushing motion toward me. She was a few feet away from me but I went flying backwards at a rapid rate, zooming for a few seconds. The next thing was I found myself taking a big breath of air and exhaling – it sounded similar to the flapping noise a horse makes with its lips.

As I was exhaling my first breath I could hear a policeman saying, "F**k! F**k! F**k! I think he's dead!"

Another one said, "He's taken a breath. I think he'll be alright."

Then I felt one of them shaking me, rocking me as I was lying on my side. Then they just walked off, closed the cell door and left me lying on the floor.

But I was not alright at all – I was completely numb all over. My head, face, tongue, arms and legs, everything, my whole body was completely numb. I thought, "Well, it's not over yet, I'm still going to die."

I had to manually breathe – I simply could not move a muscle, and my mouth was still making that strange flapping noise. Then I saw things go black again.

Next I found myself waking up again. I don't know how long I had lost consciousness but did know that I was still alive. I found I could wriggle my fingers a little bit so I kept doing it and kept up with my breathing, telling myself to stay awake or I would die. I still felt mostly numb all over, yet found I could now move my toes a little too.

I spent a very long time concentrating on staying awake and moving my fingers and it was also a very long time before I could lift my arm and move my feet and legs. I just kept hanging in there. Gradually, over time I could move a bit more and more.

It seemed a very long time before I could sit up, but eventually I crawled over to the cell bed and sat on it. I could remember everything about being carried, strangled and then arriving in heaven – the angel, all of it.

I was sitting on the bed when the cell door opened. It was the officer who had strangled me. He asked, "Do you remember what happened?"

I lied, "No, I don't," and he closed the cell door. I was too afraid to say I could remember. I feared he might do it again to stop me talking to the public about what he did.

When I look back at the experience, I can see it simply was not my time yet. God wanted me to survive and live on as he has plans for me. It also confirmed for me, that there is definitely life after death and heaven is real, even if I only got to see a small part of what it is.

It explains to me as well, that God has been helping keep me alive through all the things that have happened in my life. Some people have said I'm like a cat with nine lives. It's true that I've had many close calls, not all of which I've talked about in this book.

I am trusting that people reading this will find hope and peace and let go of their fear of death. For that's what happens when we have a firm belief there is life after death, and from seeking and finding God and accepting Jesus Christ as our Saviour.

Glory be to God!

Finding my glasses

A year after my psychosis began, when I was 31, there came a day when I ended up in hospital in a coma from an overdose of sleeping pills. The psychosis was still freaking me out and I had suffered enough and just wanted to die.

When I came out of my coma, I had a vision in hospital that I walked up to my grapevine, reached in and found my glasses, which I had lost some time before. I also had a vision that a nurse wanted to weigh me and in the vision I saw my weight on the scales was 84.7kgs.

The doctor had informed my mother that she was not to get her hopes up, as I was not expected to come out of the coma – in fact I was not expected to make it through the night and that if I did survive and come out of the coma, I could be blind and a mentally retarded vegetable. Furthermore, I could also have severe internal organ damage and my life expectancy would be short.

However, I did come out of the coma. My eyes were rather blurry and my mind unclear at first. It was like I was in the middle of the white cloud again and I thought the nurses and my sister were angels. It took some hours before I felt back into reality again. Before that, I even asked the doctor if he was God.

Anyway, they took an x-ray and conducted blood-tests and found that I had no internal organ damage, no brain damage, and my eyes came right as well. The doctor told me I had taken enough drugs to kill two people and I must be like a weed – very hard to kill.

The truth is, the doctors were baffled at my recovery. God must have been working away in me for me to survive this ordeal and not be harmed as the doctors expected.

The next day a nurse wanted to weigh me, so I stepped on to her scales and we found I was 84.7 kgs, just as in the vision I had had the night before. She said, "That's the weight you told me last night when I asked you if you knew what your weight was."

When I got home from the hospital, I was about to go in through my back door when I remembered the vision I had after coming out of the coma, regarding my glasses and my grapevine.

Now my grapevine is about 40 feet long and about seven feet tall. I just walked up to it, about half-way along and reached my hand into it, about an arm's length. I felt something, so closed my hand around it, and lo and behold, it was my missing pair of glasses.

I have found that with God all things are possible. Also, if you believe in your heart that you can do supernatural things, then you will begin to experience these happenings more and more.

Uncle Mike's boat

When I was a boy and we first arrived in New Zealand to live, we stayed at my Uncle Mike's place for a few months. I was 11 at the time, and his daughter, my cousin Pam was then only three.

I loved my Uncle Mike as he took an interest in me and we would chat together. He also told me wise things and took me fishing at the jetty and on his big launch. He introduced me to Sea Scouts as I showed a great enthusiasm for boating, and I became one of their leaders.

Later on, I bought my own little 9-foot sailing boat that I had saved up for – however it did not come with a trailer. Uncle Mike heard of this and surprised me by giving me a boat trailer that was sitting out the back of his house. I was delighted, and after sanding it down, repainted it.

By this time I was 21 and studying Chinese medicine and acupuncture. Uncle Mike looked through my textbooks and decided I was intelligent enough as I was studying and passing my exams. Then he said he wanted me to come and work for him at Bendon Underwear so that he would be able to spend more time on his boat. He and his two friends had started Bendon and it was now a large company. I was going to be placed in a top position and replace him while he was away on his boat.

I said I would think about it, as I was in the middle of my studies and wanted to finish what I had started. He said that if I worked for him, he would make me richer than in my wildest dreams. However, I decided to finish my degree. This decision would become one of my life's regrets.

Later, when I was 25 and practising as an acupuncturist, he rang me to tell me he had set up a lunch date with Elle Macpherson. He wanted me to join them as Elle wanted to meet me. She was their model for Bendon underwear as well as being a supermodel. I was told that her personality and smile could captivate a whole room full of people.

However, I was flat out with my acupuncture practice and wanted to change the day of the lunch date, but they could not, so I declined the invitation. I should have gone along, as who knows where that might have taken me, and Uncle Mike may have offered me a position at Bendon once again.

In May 2001, three weeks before I had my psychosis and break down, I drove to Auckland to visit him. He was dying of cancer and I wanted to see him before that happened. I told him my stories of blowing up my boat in Lake Rotorua and my Great White shark encounter. He told me they were things I would never forget.

He asked me if I had a boat of my own. I told him I didn't. He said, "Would you like me to leave you my boat when I go?"

I said, "Wow, I would love that and be so grateful Uncle." He went on to say he would leave me the marina berth as well, and I could sell his Auckland marina and buy one in Tauranga to park the boat at. I could not believe my ears!

His 48-foot launch was fairly new – it cost him $1,300,000 and the marina berth about $300,000. A marina berth in Tauranga was a lot cheaper, so I would have been able to pay off my house mortgage with the difference in price.

I was sad that Uncle Mike was going to die soon and I told him so. However, I was delighted he was going to leave me his boat and marina. It was awesome that he wanted to do something so nice for me and I felt that God was working within him.

About 12 months went by before my uncle died. It was such a loss for me, I always looked up to him and still remember the wise things he would say to me.

So naturally I waited with anticipation for a few months to hear the news that his 48-foot boat was now mine and that I needed to come and get it. However, this was not to be.

I eventually rang his wife, my Aunt Carol and she said she did remember this arrangement. However, her daughter Pam had complained about it after her dad passed away. She wanted to sell the boat, and the marina berth and keep the money.

I could not believe my ears. Uncle Mike would have made sure she got plenty of his money. He would not have left her out. I felt she was being greedy and selfish. Aunt Carol said, "I am sorry, Adrian, it is just how things turned out."

I was gutted. Uncle Mike had left me his boat out of the kindness of his heart and Pam had snatched it away. It felt like she had stolen it off me.

Some 14 years later, in Feb 2016 my Aunty Carol also passed away, from lung cancer. Now Pam has inherited the rest of the family assets and money, and I can tell you that now she is worth a fortune. The family home was worth a few million, plus there are millions in investments.

I spoke with Pam on the phone after her mum passed away, and told her some stories about her father and his friendship with me. Then I went on to say how he had left me his boat and marina. She replied saying that it would be nice if we still had the boat. Then she said she had company and had to go right away and hung up before I could say good bye. That just revealed to me she was feeling guilty and wanted to avoid any discussion about it.

I have found this to be very hard to get over and it has really got to me at times over the last 14 years. I know that by forgiving someone we can get some peace and move on, and I have done so over the years, however in this case I have found that forgiving is a difficult, ongoing process. Thoughts would well up and then it would affect me. I continue to forgive Pam whenever this happens, but I must say it is not at all easy.

I forgive you Pam. God bless you. Amen.

(My relatives names in this chapter have been changed to avoid embarrassment.)

Cracking the safe

One afternoon at my friend Bill's house I was in his hot spa pool. While talking with him he mentioned his safe. Some numbers came into my mind and I wondered if they were for the safe.

I said, "Bill, what would you say if I could open your safe in five seconds?"

He laughed and said, "That sounds similar to your Lotto Powerball stories."

I said, "Come on then, let me try." We went to the safe and I punched in the numbers I had in my head. Plus, I chose one of the two buttons at the base of the key pad – a choice of A or B. The safe beeped and a green light came on. So I tried the door on the safe and it opened.

Bill could not believe his eyes, and reacted, "No way, that's impossible! How on earth did you do that?"

I will say that I am not psychic all the time, it comes and goes. If I consciously try, it comes in different intensities and accuracy. When I'm properly tuned in however, things come through with precise accuracy.

I don't know why God gave me this gift, I just know that I have it.

My lottery predictions begin

I made my first lottery prediction at age 30, when my troubles began. However, it really took off a few years later at the age of 34. I was giving my friend Diane a reading at the time. She had invited me over for the night and had cooked me a nice dinner.

Sometime after dinner and her reading, we went off to bed. While lying in bed with the light off, I was telling her about my experience with Jesus when I was 25. She said that while I was telling her about it, my eyes were glowing bright white. That scared her, so she got out of bed and left the room.

Then, lying in bed, I prayed for my finances to be abundant. I explained in prayer how I had lost everything, and had been through so much mentally and emotionally. I asked God and the Lord Jesus to help me get into financial abundance and said that I would like to win the Lotto Powerball or the Big Wednesday lottery and asked for a miracle.

Then a set of six numbers came into my mind. They appeared in front of my eyes in bright fluorescent blue. I foresaw that those numbers were for the Christmas Eve draw and that it would be a six million dollar draw and the Powerball number would be 6.

I then had another set of numbers come into my mind, and again they appeared in fluorescent blue. I remembered them as being the same set of numbers I had seen in the sky, back in 2001 at age 30 while being arrested. I forecast those numbers for a Big Wednesday draw of seven million dollars, and lots of prizes, including a silver Porsche, a boat, a holiday bach and more. I also predicted at that time, the numbers would come up in about six months time from now.

Yet again I saw third set of numbers, just as before. My prediction this time was that those were also for a Big Wednesday draw of three million dollars, a Porsche and all the extra prizes.

A fourth set also came up in fluorescent blue, which were for a 17 million dollar Powerball draw which should come up sometime close to the six month mark. Then another, and these numbers I predicted were for a one million dollar Powerball draw.

Then a final set came to me, but what was different about this set, was that the numbers were up on the wall. I knew that those were for a 20 million dollar draw and it was to be in about ten years from now and I would win it then.

Suddenly I felt a powerful wave of the Holy Spirit. I called out to Diane, "Do you know anyone called Tania and Clinton?"

She replied she didn't. So I explained, "Well, I've never heard of them either, but for some reason I think the day will come when I give them two million dollars." I added, "I'll be in rehab at the time."

Stepping Stones was a name that came into my mind, so I said to her, "Have you heard of a place called Stepping Stones?" Diane said she hadn't, so I said, "It must be the name of the rehab."

As I lay in bed I thought I should really go and write down all this information before I fall asleep, but I was so sleepy I just fell off to sleep.

The next morning, I had only vague memories of my predictions and did not remember all the details. It's a bizarre kind of amnesia I get after making accurate predictions like these, but later on the memories filter back into my mind.

Diane also said that during the night, she got up to go to the bathroom and was amazed and baffled when she saw wonderful bright colours swirling around on the walls in the hallway. It was something she had never experienced before.

So near and yet so far away

On Christmas Eve, some memories came filtering back into my mind regarding the numbers I had predicted for the Christmas Eve six million dollar Powerball draw that night, so I wrote them down and added Powerball 6.

The prize money of the draw matched the prediction so far, so I just had to go and get a ticket and find out if the numbers would come up perfectly. I did not have quite enough money for a ticket, so I rang my mum and told her I had a good chance of winning the Powerball that night based on some predictions I had made a few months ago. She said she might go down to the store and get the ticket for me, so I told her the numbers.

Well anyway, I watched the draw on TV that night and wrote down the numbers as they came up. When I went and checked them, lo and behold they matched perfectly, all seven numbers. I was so excited and rang my mum, only to find that she had not gone and got the ticket. I could not believe what I was hearing. I was shattered. However I could understand that in her mind she could not believe I was able to predict the lottery. But for me, I knew within my heart that it was real and I had predicted my first lottery draw.

People usually believe only what they've experienced themselves. I told my father and he didn't believe me either and said some negative things to me.

I do not let it get to me when people don't believe such things – I just know within myself that such things are real and absolutely possible to do.

A week before the Christmas Eve draw, a woman I knew rang me and asked if she could have the numbers I had told her about previously, regarding the Christmas draw. I just gave them to her and asked if she wanted the Powerball number as well. She said, "No, it's OK thanks" and then changed the subject.

Well, she would have at least won a First Division prize, and if she had said 'Yes' to me giving her the Powerball number also, she would also have won the huge six million Powerball jackpot. Still, she would have won a lot of money with the First Division prize, and good on her. I phoned her but she did not answer the phone or call me back. She probably didn't want to part with any of her winnings.

God is not pleased

In February, I ended up at a house drinking with three guys and they wanted me to give them a reading. I started off with small stuff and got their interest, and therefore they believed I was psychic. I then predicted that in ten days time, ten tourists in a white van travelling from Auckland to Hamilton would crash head-on into a truck and all be killed. I also predicted three sets of lottery numbers, but then realized I had seen them before in fluorescent blue a few months back.

One of them asked what the numbers were again as he wanted to write them down. So I gave him the numbers for the three million dollar Big Wednesday draw that also had all the prizes. I told him it would be in twelve weeks time. He said, "Wow, I'm going to start getting the numbers right away."

(There is more to tell yet about this night's events, however twelve weeks later I was online and decided to check the site for the Big Wednesday draws. I saw they were the numbers I had given him and it was won in Whangamata, the place where the man was from. I therefore believed he had won that Big Wednesday prize.)

Later in the night, while I was drinking and predicting with those three guys, they decided from the things I had said that I was an amazing psychic, but felt my prediction of the people crashing in the van had come from an evil source and they wanted to get rid of me.

I said I had to go and got up from my chair. But then a fight broke out between us. I was doing OK until one of them smashed the whisky bottle over my head, shattering it. Then they grabbed me and took me out to their car and said they would take me home, but I wasn't convinced.

They drove right past the road that would take me home, so I said, "Hey, where are we going?"

They told me they were going to bury me up on their mate's farm. So I decided it was life or death and had to jump from the car. I opened the door, but one of them grabbed my clothing and said, "He's trying to get away." Then came a louder sound from the Holden V8 motor – the car was speeding up, but I did not care it was doing about 70km per hour, I jumped from the car onto the road. I then crawled over to the foot path and lay there. The car turned around and one of the guys got out and spoke with me. We had a few words then he got back in the car and they drove off.

A few minutes later a spirit man appeared to be walking towards me. He grabbed my hair, lifting up my head and looking in my eyes and said, "It won't be long now. You're f**ked." Then he walked off and disappeared after taking about five steps away from me.

I was amazed that he had physical strength. It seemed to be the same spirit man I encountered on the driveway a few years earlier, the one I call Satan.

Sometime later, while I was still lying there on the footpath, two policemen saw me and took me to the police station in their patrol car to ask a few questions about these men. On the way I said to the police, "A man died of head injuries in Waihi tonight." Soon after I said that, it came over the police radio. They were amazed that I had told them this before even they found out.

After arriving at the station they asked if I could see anything else. I told them that in ten days time, ten tourists will die driving from Auckland to Hamilton. Their white van would hit a truck.

I heard God speak to me while I was telling the police about the people that would die in the van crash. He said to me, "Adrian, what are you doing?"

I replied, "I'm just showing these police what I can do."

God then said, "I would not do that if I were you." Yet I carried on talking to the police.

Then God said, "Well, that is the last you will hear from me for a long time." My stomach sank, as I realised God was not pleased with me.

Then a set of numbers appeared on the police station wall under the clock, again in fluorescent blue. They were the last set of numbers I had predicted. I predicted again that they were for a 20 million dollar draw and the Powerball number would be 1 or 6. I had now seen this set of numbers three times and felt that I would win.

I end up in rehab

Ten days later the ten tourists hit the truck and all died – my details were spot on, exactly as the news report described.

However, I wrongly predicted the timing of the Powerball draw. I calculated the date to win would be the 18th of June 2016. That day came and went and I did not win.

I decided to keep trying the numbers for a while, thinking that when the Jackpot reaches 20 million I might still win – maybe my timing would not be out by much, especially given that I predicted it ten years before.

I had witnessed five sets of lottery numbers come up in real life, in a period of about six or seven months. And as I would get closer to a draw, somehow the memory of the blue numbers would come into my mind. It's bizarre, I tell you. This is common when I make any prediction – later, near to the time it's going to happen, the memory of the prediction re-enters my mind.

For one of the lottery draws, my brother went halves with me in a ticket. I filled out two coupons and said we needed two tickets. I was not well at the time as I still had concussion from my night jumping from the guys in the white V8 Holden. I was therefore struggling to remember what set of numbers we needed for this draw.

He said, "Pick one coupon. We're just getting one ticket," even though he had enough money for two. He said he wanted to buy some chicken wings. I tried telling him to not worry about chicken wings today, as this was far more important and money wouldn't be a problem after today when we've won.

He said "No." So I just purchased the one ticket then held onto both of the coupons and took them to the car. While he was eating his chicken wings I had a flashback and a memory return. I looked at the ticket and the coupons, and realized the numbers I wanted were not on the ticket, but were on the other coupon that we did not get a ticket for. I told him, "We must go and get this second ticket Gabriel. I have remembered the numbers that we need to get." But he would not, so I said, "Well, don't cry to me if I'm correct. It's possible this is a chance in a lifetime for you".

The next day we went out in the car and decided to go and check the results. I walked into the shop and asked for a print out and took it back to the car. After checking the numbers from the results print out I said, "These are the numbers I wanted to get for last night's draw, but we have a serious problem, the numbers are not on our ticket, they are on the coupon I wanted to get for the second ticket."

He reacted, "Bullshit, I don't believe that!"

I responded, "I told you bro, and we can't turn the clock back and fix it." I looked for the Lotto coupons and found them and there they were all correct. I showed him and he compared the numbers with the results. He then said, "Shit, I can't believe it. I wish I'd believed you".

You know, for people who believe in the supernatural, the golden rule is to truly believe it is possible to predict the future. If one truly believes without any doubts, then it's possible to do. It may take time but it will happen.

Gabriel was gutted over missing out on this Lotto Powerball draw and three years later took his own life over a woman. He had a broken heart, but a few days before he died he said to me, "It sucks that we missed out on the money that day with the Lotto." It made me wonder if there was more to it than a broken heart over a woman.

For one reason or another I personally missed out on five winning lottery draws – two big Wednesday draws and three Lotto Powerball draws. I witnessed them happen in real life, or checked the results afterward.

One of them was for a 17.5 million-dollar Powerball draw. I thought this draw was close enough to bet on. My prediction was for a 17 million dollar draw, so I decided, "I'm doing this myself and I'm getting tickets." I had the money, no problem there, I was sitting at a bar having a beer and the Lotto shop was right across the road. So I got up from my chair and started walking over to get my tickets.

That was when I had flashbacks of the spirit man I thought could be Satan. I also thought of John, a Jehovah Witness who had been telling me that my predictions for the Powerball were evil and that doom would come to me. Plus I had doubts and fears come into me and I thought maybe I should think this over.

So I went back to the bar and drank some more beer and did some thinking. I ended up doing too much thinking, drinking and over analysing things that it left me confused as to what to do. However, I did walk over to the store a second time, but there was a big line of people wanting to buy tickets, so I thought I'd come back later, but I didn't.

I really wanted to get the tickets and the numbers, as I wanted to show the Lotto Commission and the public that I could correctly predict and it was not just a random win.

This began a long-term depression, because the numbers did come up, but again I had not got my tickets. This draw was the hardest for me to get over, as I had the money at the time and I also had time to get the tickets. It would have been awesome indeed, instead I suffered a lot of regret.

Casting out doubt and fear is another golden rule, but it was a hard way for me to learn this.

More supernatural experiences

About five years later, when I was 40, I was driving with my brother-in-law Brad when some Lotto numbers came into my mind. Soon afterward, he pulled into a car park by some shops as he wanted to visit his mother at her work. I spotted a Lotto shop and went in and bought a ticket with the numbers that had popped into my mind. They did come up, but I had only five out of the six numbers correct. I was just one number short of winning a million dollars.

Another time I was at a meeting of the Spiritual Club in Tauranga. They had raffle tickets for two big hampers full of goodies. We sat down in our seats and looked at our tickets. I said to my friend Diane, "You will need the numbers 12 or 82 to win. At the end of the meeting the raffle was drawn and they called out the numbers 12 and 82 as the winning tickets.

One day I may still win Lotto Powerball. However, as mentioned earlier, the last set of numbers in blue that I had predicted was for ten years' time which I worked out to be the 16th of June 2016. However, that day came and went and I did not win the draw, which turned out to be for 22 million.

The same night that I predicted all six sets of numbers in fluorescent blue, I also predicted that in ten years' time I would be at a rehab place called Stepping Stone where there would be a Tania and a Clinton. As I write this book I am actually at this very rehab. I'm waiting for the Powerball draw to reach 20 million and I will try again. Furthermore I predicted that I would give them two million of the 20 million-dollar draw. Well, I believe I still have a chance and may still win that one.

I have also predicted many tragedies and events. At the police stations in both Rotorua and Tauranga, some of the police have witnessed me making predictions they have then seen happen in real life on the news on TV etc. I'm happy to take a polygraph (lie detector) test done on me to prove to the world that my book is the whole truth and nothing but the truth, so help me God.

I would welcome this.

How to do predictions yourself

I am hoping my strange story can open people's eyes and minds. One needs to believe and cast out all doubts and fears. Once you believe, you open yourself up to experiencing your own predictions and your own supernatural experiences.

People often ask me how I do what I do and wish they could do it too. Often it's because I've just told them their phone number, or date of birth, or something only they would know.

Also, quite a few people have witnessed me predicting events and tragedies, and then they've seen them happen themselves with their own eyes or on the news, etc.

Don't limit yourself. It is all very possible. The golden rule is to truly believe that it's possible for you to achieve. Also it's very important to cast out doubts and fears.

Good luck and good fortune everyone with your own predictions.

Some more significant predictions

I have predicted a lot of things – however, here I will write only about the more significant ones.

One of my predictions was that Sir Peter Blake, a famous New Zealand sailor, would be shot by eight natives while overseas on his yacht. I told the Rotorua police this and asked them to write down the details. In fact I gave them even more details, like where to look for the murderers, and how they would go about the shooting, and they wrote it all down.

After it happened, the police took notice of what I had predicted and used the information I gave to assist them. They sent a special task force to investigate and to arrest the eight natives, which they charged with murder.

I predicted in great detail the 9/11 Twin Tower attack in New York. I said Bin Laden would be responsible for jumbo jets flying into the Twin Towers in New York in four months' time and that 3500 people would die, including 300 firemen and 50 police officers. I predicted this on the 10 May 2001.

Around 2007 I predicted a man named Anthony Dixon would die on the day of his court case in a police holding cell at court. He would be trying to get an appeal and to get off on an insanity plea. I told the Tauranga police that this would happen.

That same night I predicted and told the same police that there would be a bush fire in Australia. I told them where and that 200 would die and there would be 900 burn victims. All these things happened afterwards.

Near the end of 2011, I predicted that 11 people would die in a hot air balloon accident in a town next to Masterton called Carterton. What I specified was that they would fly into power lines then plunge to the ground, and that two people would fall from the balloon basket while it was still dangling from the power lines.

I also predicted that a Russian satellite would fall from its orbit and crash into the sea in three days time.

All these events happened in real life exactly as I predicted them. They are the major significant predictions of tragedies I have made over the last 15 years. It's all true and all real.

Somehow, things and events take place in the universal energy field in the spirit realm that can be predicted well before the event takes place in real time, as I have done.

I often say to people, "Time is not what you think it is, and if you don't believe it's possible, then you need to think again." It's reality.

I have had so many experiences of predicting things and seeing them happen in real time in real life that I know for a fact that some things don't happen at random.

I'm not saying that everything is predestined to happen beforehand, such as the bird flying over your head, or the dog running over to get his bone. But from my experience I can assure you that things don't always happen by accident or at random.

They are set in place in the future, in the universal energy field and they will happen when the right time presents itself. This I why I say to people "Time is not what you think it is."

Not all things are bad in this energy field. There are all sorts of good things going to happen as well, including the lottery numbers.

Trust me, I know for a fact this is all real.

Sensing danger

I like to trust my instincts – my gut feeling about things. I've learned it pays to in life, as I've made mistakes and run into trouble by not taking notice of my gut feeling about a situation. Many refer to it as the Sixth Sense. I've had too many experiences of this to write about them all.

Some times, when driving a car, I sense danger and slow down, only to see someone coming around the corner on the wrong side of the road, overtaking another vehicle. This allows me to take the necessary evasive action.

I'm a true believer in sensing danger and often instinctively know when it is around. Here is one example. I was 22 at the time, on my way to Auckland from Rotorua – about a three hour drive, for my weekly acupuncture study time. It's late at night and I'm two thirds of the way there. I'm following behind a large truck and decide to overtake it and put my foot down and off I go. I am half way through the overtaking manoeuvre when I have a vision of a car. Yet I cannot see any headlights coming towards me.

Everything seemed fine and there was no obvious reason for concern. However, I quickly decided I should abort the overtake manoeuvre because the vision I saw must have been for a good reason. So I brake hard, and when the rear of the truck lines up with the front of my car, I pull in behind the truck. Then within two seconds, a car zooms past me at high speed from the opposite direction. I could tell it was speeding as I heard its engine revving hard. The car had no headlights on.

I felt so relieved and pleased that I had taken notice of my vision and taken immediate action. I think the driver was either drunk or suicidal, or both. Had I carried on passing the truck I would almost certainly have been killed in a head on crash.

Trust in God to protect you and trust your gut feelings if you sense danger. Halleluiah, God is good.

God, me and Satan

One of the things I have long wondered about is – why did I have a psychosis and maybe have to deal with Satan personally and lose everything and get left in 15 years of torment? The 'Perfect Storm' as I often call it.

The first six years were like a nightmare that I could not wake up from, even though I was awake. I felt like I was mentally, emotionally and financially emptied – living a totally alien life.

If it was not Satan I was dealing with, then it was one of his main henchmen. I cannot remember everything he said to me at the beginning, but he's an expert at terrorising people. He tells you things that will happen to you soon and also in years to come. Some of it comes true, leaving you thinking the rest of the things will also happen. It leaves you living in fear for years. His main goal is to destroy you and lead you to commit suicide.

Sometimes I feel that God handed me over to Satan and let him have his way with me, so that God could see how well I would cope with it all – such as being stripped of all my possessions and my income, etc.

What I do know, is that if someone is at the beginning of a spiritual breakthrough, Satan hates it and tries to ruin it, and to destroy you and your progress.

Did my 15 year storm of mental and emotional trauma, along with my financial ruin, my poverty and my depression have anything to do with God punishing me, or was he trying to teach me something? Or was it that God was not pleased with me and was allowing Satan to destroy me? The book of Job in the Bible tells a story of God allowing Satan to have his way with Job.

Another thing I often think about, is when the Great White shark was swimming towards me at the age of 29, I prayed and promised God that if he saved me from the shark, I would devote myself to Him and not sin anymore, and do His will from that point onwards. The truth is, I did not honour that commitment as well as I could have. I did not try hard enough or devote my daily life to Him as I should have.

Now I choose to devote every minute of my day to God and to Jesus and to the Holy Spirit. It is the main priority in my life.

Not long before I had my psychosis and breakdown in May 2001, I wrote God a letter saying that I wanted to reach my full potential in Christ, like Jesus himself did, and that I wanted God to speed up the process. I said I wanted to reside in the highest realm in heaven with the Lord Jesus.

I also offered to battle Satan in person, and challenged God to test me. I went outside and read my letter aloud a few times and then burnt what I had written.

Be careful what you ask God for.

I have been a spiritual man all my life, but did not always keep God my main focus and priority in daily life. I would do God's will in many ways, but not in all ways.

Once you invite Jesus and God into your life, they will change you from the inside out and you will become Christ-like.

In addition to this it is important to sincerely try to do God's will. Praise to the Lord.

Is evolution fact or is God our creator?

It is my belief that God is the great creator of all things. The earth rotates around the sun at just the right distance, making the temperature just perfect for life here on planet earth. In my opinion this cannot be by chance. If we were any further away from the sun we would freeze. If any closer we wouldn't be able to survive. If the earth was 10% larger or 10% smaller, life as we know it wouldn't be possible.

This planet tilts its axis, giving us summer and winter. None of the other planets are tilted like ours at 23°. This angle allows the sun's rays to touch every part of the earth's surface over the course of a year as the earth circles the sun. If there was no tilt to the axis, the poles would accumulate enormous masses of ice and the centre of the earth would become so hot we could not stand it.

Without the moon it would be impossible for us to live on this earth. If the moon deflected off its orbit, all life would cease. It acts like a cleaner, to clean up the oceans and the shores. Without the tides created by the moon, our harbours and shores would become one huge stench pool of garbage and be impossible to live near.

It seems that an increasing number of scientists who formerly believed in evolution, have now decided, after much research, that evolution does not stack up. Many of them have become Christians and now believe God to be the great creator of all things on earth. Also it is reported that 90% of the world's astronomers believe in God.

Many of the world's greatest thinkers believe that God not only exists but that He created the universe and its inhabitants.

One thing I find difficult to believe is that dinosaurs have been around for 65 million years. One man came to give a talk at Stepping Stone Ministries where I am currently residing and told a different story. He is a teacher at a local high school and a professor in some area of science. He has found evidence that indicates that dinosaurs have been here for a much shorter time. He also said that some dinosaur bones were recently found with DNA still alive and they dated back only 600 years.

Furthermore, why is the temperature so precise that everything lives and flourishes on earth? There are so many different kinds of creatures and varieties of plant life, how is it possible they all evolved from something such as bacteria or some other creature. And where is the evidence of any half-evolved creatures? If you look at rabbits for example, they are all perfectly the same – there are no rabbits that seem to be in a different stage of evolution or transformation. This example can be extended to all living creatures.

Finally, if animals evolved from bacteria, or a small sea creature, how would their DNA know how to evolve into a tiger or any other animal? There are all the internal organs and a brain and so many million intricate details needed to form and to function.

Think about it deeply. God just has to be the original creator of all things.

Fighting

I've been in several fights in my life and I've won some and lost some. Sometimes neither side won. For a few I've felt God was definitely there with me and helping me.

I try to avoid fighting whenever possible, however at times I have needed to engage with someone as a matter of self-defence, but I do prefer to avoid this if at all possible.

Here is one situation I found myself in and where there seemed no way out. I thought I was about to lose my life.

My friend Greg and I had gone to a party. Things were going along fine and we were enjoying the live band and a massive bonfire. That is until about 20 gang members crashed it.

It didn't take long before trouble started. Different ones would come over to us and challenge us to fight. I said, "No, we're not here to fight, we just want to have a good time." Then they would come over and say, "I've got a problem with you, so let's have a rumble." I tried saying, "Well, I'm just having a drink right now, how about we have one together and a chat instead." Different ones came over, saying different things, but we tried to avoid fighting.

I felt things were about to turn very nasty, so said to my friend Greg, "Say a prayer and repent and apologise to God for your sins." At that Greg cracked up laughing, which got me laughing too.

However, I said my own prayer to God and to Jesus. However it seemed this prayer was not working when a few of the gang came over and said, "Take a look around you. You're not going anywhere. We have the exits blocked off."

They said they were going to beat us up, kill us, then take us out to sea and feed us to the sharks. They gathered around us in a circle, so there was no escape possible.

I said to Greg, "Go back-to-back with me, and fight hard and I'll see you on the other side if we don't make it out alive."

I then said to the gang members, "Who wants to go first? I'm going to really bust up the first one and do a lot of damage before I die." I added, "God is on my side, so if you want some bad karma, go right ahead. So, who's going first?"

There was murmuring as they spoke amongst themselves saying "You go first," and "No, why me, you go first." Another said he felt something very strongly, saying. "I think we should let these guys go." There was more talk regarding this, so then I said, "Well, I'm off to have another drink," and walked right through them and got a drink for myself and Greg. None of them wanted to fight me.

They left us alone after that and even drank with us and talked. I was asked if I wanted to join their gang, but I said "No thanks guys."

They didn't want us to leave however, and insisted we drink with them until the sun came up. We decided we should go along with their request.

Greg felt lucky to be alive and thanked me for helping save him. God helped me survive that night alright. No doubt about it.

Bo is out of air

One nice sunny morning, my friend Bill and I, with his two sons Bo and Chad, went out on Bill's boat to do some diving. Bo had just completed his dive certificate and was keen to go on his first sea dive with his boys.

We anchored in about 22 metres (70 feet) of water off the coast and Bo and I got suited up in our dive gear, then over the side we went. We descended down to the bottom and found the type of rocks that crayfish like to live in.

I was enjoying my dive and had bagged three large crays. I checked my dive gauge and saw I had plenty of air left, so I was keen for more crays. Then suddenly Bo swam over to me and gestured the cut throat signal to tell me he was out of air. Instead of waiting for me to take a breath, then pass him my regulator, he just grabbed it from my mouth, took a few breaths then handed it back to me so I could take a breath.

I purged the regulator to clear it of water, took a couple more breaths and handed it to Bo. I then reached for and found my emergency back-up regulator and put that in my mouth. Things seemed to be going OK now that both of us had air, so we set off for the surface.

However, Bo panicked and swam very fast and did not dump any air from his floatation device. He had no reason to panic and swim fast for the surface. I had hold of his dive belt and tried to slow us down by not flipping my fins and by dumping all of the air from my BCD (Buoyancy Control Device) but he kept rushing, racing to get to the top.

I thought of letting go of him, as I was in danger of getting the bends by coming up from such a depth at this speed, after being loaded with nitrogen. But I hung onto him so he could keep breathing from my tank. We broke the surface with Bo in distress. I was very worried we would both get the bends. Also, I noticed I had dropped my dive bag with my three crays in it.

So I changed tanks and went back down to find my dive bag. In addition, I wanted to recompress the nitrogen in my body, hopefully lessening my chance of getting the bends. I could not find my dive bag, despite having a very good look around – I even found myself in 25 metres of water looking for it.

I decided to go resurface, but stop half way and wait a few minutes to decompress to help lessen my chances of the bends. Then I came up to the surface. Thankfully neither of us got the bends, but we called it quits on diving for the day.

Bo is one of several I've saved in my rather chequered life thus far. I saved Bo that day and I saved my two friends when my boat blew up. I also saved my friend Greg one night when petrol spurted on him and he caught seriously on fire. I had to jump on him and smother out the flames, even though petrol was on me too.

It's a good feeling to know that I saved those guys, and I know God gave me the courage to do it.

Bo doesn't even like me, yet I still chose to save him, as I would want to be saved. The glory is for God, not for me.

The 1987 market crash

I am 17 years old at the time of this story and in my last year of high school. There is a job opportunity called out in assembly for a Junior Stock Broker. I decide to look into it and arrange an interview. The first interview went well and I'm called back for a second one. I also sit an examination to determine my personality traits and IQ level.

I get the job and am due to start in the new year after leaving school. I'm to have my own office and a personal trainer for two years. I'm delighted and can't wait to start.

However things didn't turn out well – the stock market crashed in 1987 and my contract was abruptly terminated. It was a shame I didn't get to be a stock broker due to the market crash. As you can imagine I was gutted.

But I had to move on, so I went up to Auckland and got a job working on building sites. One of them was an 11 storey high building. When I arrived for work one Monday morning, I walked around the corner of the building and to my surprise there was the body of a man lying face up on a large log. I walked up to him for a closer inspection and found he was dead. His eyes were still open and blood was coming out of his mouth. He had on a business shirt, the top was open and there was blood on it.

I walked back around the building and said to my work buddy, "Bro, there's a dead guy around the corner." He didn't believe me, so I said "Go and look for yourself." I followed him as he went to look. He saw and reacted with, "Shit, you're telling the truth" and as we stood next to the dead man, he closed his eyes with his fingers.

As I was the first to find the dead man, the police made me sit and wait in the smoko shed on my own, with an officer guarding the door. After quite some time, I was allowed out and was then interrogated by detectives. They questioned me as to whether I knew the man and whether he owed me money, and a number of other questions.

After the investigation they cleared me and told me the man had lost everything in the stock market crash and had jumped to commit suicide. The man obviously took his life because he could not face living without lots of money. It seems he did not want to start again and rebuild his life and wealth – a shame really. I've felt suicidal at times myself and even survived a couple of attempts.

But, 'Never give up,' I say.

The UFO puzzle

Not many people believe in UFOs – that's because most people don't believe something unless they've seen it for themselves. I think they are real, as I have had some experiences of UFO sightings.

One of those was when I was 24. My mother phoned me on my cell-phone to tell me she was watching some strange lights descending slowly over Mount Ngongataha near Rotorua. She says "I can see all this from my lounge window," so I told her I would come over and take a look.

I drove to my mother's house and waited patiently. Then I observed several different lights slowly moving down from the sky. They would move down, then stop and remain stationary, as if they were trying to be discreet and not be noticed. Then five minutes later they would move down in the sky some more, then sit stationary again.

So I drove up the mountain with my girlfriend Melanie and my brother Gabriel in the car. They were too scared to get out of the car ,so I got out and went to look around myself.

I saw red lights in the distance, then suddenly they zoomed at great speed closer to me. I even got to see that one flying object had a ring of lights under its belly.

I also saw another one with a blue light and it lit up the ground as it moved slowly along. It appeared to have a windscreen that shone bright white, as if a light was on inside the craft. There was not a sound to be heard. It was definitely not a plane or a chopper, it had to be some kind of alien craft.

There were other cars up the mountain by the time we left, all looking to see if they could spot something.

That night Melanie went out to her car to get something and came running back inside screaming that there was a large bright blue light and something hovering above her outside.

Another sighting came when I was 27. This time I was with Melanie and five others. We had gone camping and water skiing for the weekend at a place south of Rotorua. We were enjoying a hot pool in a natural hot spring named Butchers Pool at Reporoa. That was when I looked over and saw two red lights in the sky travelling side by side.

I said to the others, "Take a look at this" and pointed at the lights. One of the lights then did a few zigzags in the sky and zoomed off at great speed into the distance. Then the other did the same thing. They were going faster than jet planes fly.

Melanie felt sure they were UFOs, but the others all had different opinions – such as that they were satellites or planes. They also said, "UFOs don't exist so they can't be UFOs." Well, I was sure I knew what they were – alien space craft or UFOs. To me there's just no other explanation.

Another sighting took place when I was 32. I was in Bill's outdoor spa pool at night and saw a white light travelling in the sky, moving slowly along. Its light went out then reappeared instantly, a long way further along in the direction it had been travelling. I pointed it out to Bill and it did it again while Bill was watching. It was slowly cruising along, then its light would go out and instantly reappear a long distance further away.

I thought it had to be a UFO and Bill agreed with me, even though he couldn't really believe what he was seeing.

Again the craft in the sky did the same thing, and Bill agreed with me that no jet plane could do what this craft was doing. It was simply travelling far too fast to be a jet plane. My friend Bill began to panic and said he was going inside the house to hide, in case he was in danger.

The next morning, I jumped back into the spa pool for a morning dip. The day was dawning and the sun had just started to bring light. I looked over to my left and couldn't believe my eyes. There was a space craft and it was an awesome sight indeed. It was at the end of Bill's farm driveway, about 200 metres (650 feet) away, hovering above some tall trees on his neighbour's land. This craft was silver and was approximately 18 metres (60 feet) or more in length and appeared to be a disc shape. I could see the ends or sides of the craft curved downwards.

As I said, I couldn't believe my eyes – it was just such an amazing, awesome sight to see, and in daylight. I jumped out of the spa and ran to wake Bill up, but by the time I got him out of bed and to his bedroom window, the craft was gone. He said, "Well, I believe I saw a UFO with you last night, so I believe you just saw one".

It happened again when I was in the Coromandel at Whitianga, having a holiday at my friend Greg's house. We had been into town one evening for a bite to eat and a couple of drinks. We then went to the bottle store and purchased a box of beer and headed back down the road to his house. We then decided to walk down to the beach in the dark and opened our box of beer.

Suddenly a bright white light came on. It was only about 50 metres (160 feet) away and above the shoreline. Both of us were startled. Greg said it had to be a UFO and that he had seen one before. Then it cruised slowly in the sky above the sea, not that high up and close enough to make me worry. I was concerned, as one never knows what could happen. Suddenly its lights went out then instantly reappeared 300 metres (1000 feet) away. Next it flashed its lights on and off at least six times, then left its lights on and continued to cruise along slowly.

Greg was excited to see this UFO, and so was I. We drank our beers and told each other stories. It sure was an exciting night to remember.

I've seen these UFO lights a number of times now. They are usually red or white, or occasionally blue. They can be less dramatic and just suddenly appear and move along for a while then vanish. They can also be there but have their lights out, so you cannot see them. Sometimes I feel as if they are watching me and appear especially so I can see them. I do not know for sure, but do wonder sometimes.

If you don't believe in UFOs, I suggest you keep an open mind.

Dream or reality?

Here is a very unusual experience, but I cannot be really sure it did happen, or was just a dream.

One night, when I was 24, I went outside to check on my dog and saw a ring of red lights hovering in the sky. The lights were moving slowly. I expected to hear an engine noise but there was no noise at all and they were fairly close. They were not the blinking lights you see with aircraft either. I felt sure it was a UFO.

That same night, after I had gone to bed, I suddenly found myself sitting in a small room that had metallic walls. The door opened by sliding sideways like elevator doors do and two grey aliens appeared, standing in front of me. Sensing danger, I pushed one of them as I tried to get away. The next moment I'm hit with something like a Taser-gun, giving me an electric shock that made me fall to the floor.

Then I found myself walking down a corridor following a pretty blond alien woman. She looked human except for a smaller than usual nose and larger than usual eyes. The two grey aliens were walking behind me. They had very large, dark eyes and a spindly body. I was thinking the blond alien woman was rather attractive when she turned and said to me, "Be careful what you're thinking."

We walk through an enormous room that was full of spacecraft. They were disc shaped and metallic in colour, except three of them that resembled a modern day stealth fighter used by the US air force.

Then I'm led along another corridor into a room that had computer screens with grey aliens sitting at them. The blond woman introduces me to a tall, blond alien man who leads me to a window so I can see planet earth. He then shows me a star map on the wall and points out where they had come from. There was a pole there with a dome on the top. The alien man placed his hand on the dome and spoke and told me he could control the aircraft by placing his hand on it. He then said that one day he will return and that I will then be in need of his help. I asked when, and he replied that he could not say when, but that I would know at the time and that it would be him, coming to help me.

Then I find myself lying on a table with a bright light above me and grey aliens around me. I can see a metal rod and they insert it up my nasal passage.

The next morning, when I awake, I am having vivid flashes of memories of this encounter. My nose is bleeding heavily and I am facing the wrong way on my bed, with my feet up by my pillow. My watch battery is dead, and when I get into my car to drive to work, it won't start as the battery is flat.

All very strange indeed. So, was it a real alien abduction or just a dream?

One more alien experience for you to ponder on. This one is more recent. I was 41 and had gone to the accident and emergency department at the Tauranga hospital. I was nauseous and had been vomiting and felt delirious. After sitting in the waiting room, a nurse took me through to the examination area and left me to wait for a doctor. He came, asked me some questions and took a blood sample. I was then left to rest on the bed, waiting for the results.

As I was lying there, some grey aliens approached me and suddenly I'm paralysed and cannot move. I can see one of them next to me and I get a look at his hand. He had very long fingers. I'm wide awake, but can't move a muscle. He tells me that I will be alright and he is just helping me. He speaks to the others in a different language. I could feel his fingers moving around on my chest and abdomen. After a few minutes they left me.

I wondered how they would have been able to walk around the hospital without being noticed. Can they make themselves invisible? Can they teleport themselves back to their craft? I don't know the answers, I just know I was awake and it seemed very real.

My battle with the bottle

If you have a drinking problem, this chapter may be of help to you.

I was not only a binge drinker, but would also at times drink daily – I drank daily for nine months one time and about six months another time.

I was definitely just a binge drinker up to the age of 27. It was only when I turned 28 that I thought, "Gosh, I don't know what to do about my drinking." When I drink I can't stop until I'm drunk. I did not think I was an alcoholic. I thought alcoholics drank every day and others wore trench coats and carried a bottle in a brown paper bag.

On my 28th birthday I decided I'd had enough and agreed to go to a meeting of Alcoholics Anonymous. There I couldn't believe my ears – the stories being told were so similar to mine that I could easily relate well to what they were talking about. When I went home that night, I had already decided I was an alcoholic. I stopped drinking right away, but initially fell over and had a couple of binges. Then I sobered up for almost four years.

When I was 30, about six months after my botched medical operation that left me in so much pain, I decided that marijuana might be the answer. I thought it would help with the pain, and also calm my mind as I was stressing out with much anger and bitterness toward the surgeon.

That same year, on the 10th of May 2001, the combination of extreme stress and marijuana caused my mental breakdown and the drug-induced psychosis I wrote about in an earlier chapter. I had not drunk for about three years, and I stopped smoking pot that day.

The psychosis was ongoing, and a year later in May 2002, I attempted suicide, as I could not cope with what I was experiencing mentally. The extreme stress was daily and ongoing since I had the psychosis. I ended up on a life support machine after my friend Greg found me unconscious in my garden.

A week later I began drinking again. I just could not cope with my living hell and purchased a bottle of whisky and drank it. I plummeted into drinking a bottle of whisky a day for nine months. I just could not stop. I kept telling myself I needed it to cope with life.

After sobering up for seven months, I found myself drinking with a new girlfriend, and that led back into daily drinking, which lasted for at least six months.

I did pull out of it, but from then onwards I went back to being a binge drinker. The binges could last for two or more days, even sometimes a week or more.

I would sober up for different lengths of time and would go to AA meetings, but I was suffering mentally and emotionally as well as having depression. I would sometimes feel I could no longer cope, and that often led me to consider suicide, but then I would choose to drink instead.

It's extremely difficult to stay sober when one is suffering mentally and emotionally.

Progressing toward recovery

For a short time I was living in a park, a place I never thought I would find myself in. I did this for two months, which was enough to show me that I really had to do something about my drinking and about my life.

I went to church a few times, hoping to find a connection with God again. I had not paid him much attention during my past 15 years of psychosis. Due to my suffering mentally, emotionally and financially, and the loss of my lifestyle, I felt that God had given up on me, so I didn't keep in contact with him or try to please him in any way.

I didn't feel at first that I was finding God again by going to church, but I went a few more times anyway, hoping it would help – and God did help. It came about by my meeting with a woman at church named Tania. I discovered that she ran a Christian rehab centre called Stepping Stone Ministries, a place set up to help people just like me.

She invited me to come and stay at her ministry, a place where anyone can progress toward rehabilitation. Alcohol is forbidden there and their long term goal is the recovery from addiction of any kind.

So I went to Stepping Stone Ministries the next day, the 25th of January 2016. I have been there over 10 months now, and that is where I am writing this book. Almost everyone here is in for recovery from addiction – either drugs or alcohol or both. We all attend chapel and Bible study every day and church in town on Sundays. We do chores and afternoon jobs on the farm. I'm not sure how long I will remain there.

I have had good times in the company of others here, and it does not involve drinking. I enjoy the worship and Bible studies and gave up smoking a few months ago. Giving up smoking had seemed like an impossible task in the past, so I thought it would be extra hard this time, but it was easier than expected.

That is thanks to the help of the Lord Jesus who has taken away my craving to smoke and to drink. Turning to God is the best way to go if you need to abstain from addictions. I am attending AA meetings as well, as I do find them helpful to my recovery. Life is better in every way when God and the Lord Jesus are the main priority in one's daily life.

If you turn fully to God, He can take your desire to use alcohol away and give you peace and contentment in life, even moments of joy. I am a recovering alcoholic and living in recovery. I am living in the solution not the problem. Praise the Lord.

The Golden Rule is to not to backslide in your addiction and have just one, as that reopens the floodgates and one is back to living and fighting and suffering from their addiction.

Letting go of hatred and bitterness and forgiving those who have hurt you, and yourself also, all help you remain connected with God and allow His Spirit to live in you and help you in many ways.

May God bless all those who read this who are struggling with any addiction.

God has kept me alive

I feel God has wanted me to stay alive as he has a plan for me and he also wants me to aspire to higher spiritual growth, and eventually inherit the Kingdom of Heaven and Eternal Life.

I've had people say I'm like a cat with nine lives. Well, I've had more than my nine lives, and also several close calls with accidents that could have left me in a wheelchair.

I am grateful to God and the Lord Jesus for this protection and that I am still alive.

As mentioned earlier in the book, I have also been strangled and seemingly gone to heaven, only to be sent back by an angel and found myself so numb all over I could not move. Yet I'm still alive today. The angel in heaven told me it was not my time yet and I must go back before it is too late.

I've had two nasty car accidents, plus several near misses. I've fallen off horses over 25 times. Furthermore, I've nearly died skydiving, been shot at, had a Great White shark to deal with, and also survived a boating accident. Most of these are in this book, but there have also been other near misses I've not written about.

To me there is far more to all this than meets the eye. I feel sure God has helped keep me alive and without him I would not be here today.

Some helps to finding God

God and the Lord Jesus want everyone to seek and find them. They want to build a close relationship with you.

This may be easier than you think. You may already be closer than you realise. The spiritual realm is within your reach, more close than you may realise.

It does not have to be a long journey to find it, let alone a life-long journey. Jesus said, "Those who are first shall be last, and those who are last shall be first." The way to God our Father is through his Son, the one who is called Jesus. God has made him to be our Saviour and our only way into heaven to inherit Eternal Life.

What we must first do is to ask God for his forgiveness for our many sins – that is, for all our wrong choices and our wrong-doing. It helps to confess these to another person, as well as to God.

This shows God that we are truly repenting, or changing our mind about how we have been living. Repenting is turning our lives around and breaking old habits that do damage to ourself or to others.

We need to release and let go of all resentments, anger, bitterness and hatred. This can take time and can be an ongoing process. We have to forgive all who have caused us harm or done us wrong and leave it in God's hands to deal with it. This also takes time and can be an ongoing process, but it brings us peace and a better appreciation for how God and Jesus have also forgiven us for our sins and wrong doing. Forgiving someone does not mean you have let them be your friend, or be part of your life.

Make God and Jesus the priority in your daily life and keep up communication with them by prayer. They want a close, even an intimate relationship with you.

Remember, God knows what we are thinking and knows the intentions of our heart and our motives. We should remember this when we are going about our daily activities. So always have good intentions and good motives.

If we're genuine and have good intentions, our lives don't need to be a constant struggle. We just every day put our best foot forward and God will give us his Holy Spirit and guide us and change our thinking as to how we feel about this and that. Let him work his will within us.

If we hand our life and our will over to the care of God and do his will, He will honour us for this and help us change our thinking, and rid us of sin and our old habits and way of life.

Grab yourself a Bible and study the Word of God and practice it in your daily life. Take care not to over analyse it, as we could find ourself lacking faith that it is from God. Likewise, we should not criticise the contents of the Bible. This can stop us from experiencing God and having him change our life and our destiny. You do not want give up when you are closer to finding God than you think.

If we seek to do God's will, he will help us do it. The Bible says, "For whoever is in Christ is a new creation, the old has gone, the new has come." (2 Corinthians 5: 17)

When God touches you, you may feel waves of the Holy Spirit wash over you. In any case, you will have a sense of God's presence, of the Holy Spirit within you. Peace will come to you. Extremely powerful experiences of feeling at one with God are also possible.

This truly is the best way to live one's life and the amazing truth is, it also leads to inheriting the Kingdom of Heaven and Eternal Life.

We need to walk the narrow path of holiness and become like Jesus and not go back to our old way of life. Find a local church and go along to worship the Lord.

Do not become disheartened if you feel God is not answering your prayer immediately. His timing is always perfect.

Ask God in your prayers what his purpose is for your life.

Also, it is important to be grateful and to give thanks for things when you pray.

Beware of distractions in your daily life, such as cell phones, TV, sex, lust, Facebook, the internet, wanting a better car or a bigger house. Many things can take our focus off God and onto self.

We must be careful who we allow to be our friends and who we socialise with. The wrong people can lead us astray and bring us down on our new life journey. Other people's behaviour is contagious, so hang out with the right people and their behaviour will be a positive influence and encouragement to you.

Especially learn to say no to people who may lead you away from God. Give a firm 'No!' to any drink or drug addictions you have left behind in your past. Do not submit to peer pressure.

Do your work with love and the Holy Spirit. Pay attention to detail and do things properly and don't cut corners. Living this way leads to success.

If you are seeking a partner or wife, I suggest you choose one who feels like a friend and not one whom you only lust for. This is of prime importance. Friendship is one of the keys to a good marriage.

Never forget that cigarettes, alcohol and drugs are not only bad for us, but can also control and even destroy our life. Jesus and God want us to refuse to allow them to dictate or consume our life. If we have an addiction we will focus on that substance and it will control how we live our life.

God does not want us worshiping any other gods or idols and these can include addictions to substances. He cannot allow those who live drunken lifestyles to inherit the kingdom of God. He wants us to focus on Him rather than on drugs, or alcohol, or lust and sex.

It's very important to love God and Jesus wholeheartedly and to love our neighbour (that's all other people) as well. Be kind to all other people for Jesus sake, so that God will get the glory.

If you truly believe in Jesus as your Lord and Saviour and believe that He died for your sins and rose again three days later from being dead, then you will be saved, because of his grace, his love and his mercy for us. To be saved means to be saved from our sins, and saved to live with God forever.

However, we cannot make it into heaven just because we live a righteous life and are a good person and do not over-indulge in alcohol and do drugs. We must also believe in Jesus and ask him into our lives and repent of our sins. He is the only doorway into heaven, into his Father's kingdom.

Jesus gave us two main commandments to live by – first, to love God and Jesus and the Holy Spirit with all our heart soul and mind. And second, to love others the way that we would want to be loved, and to treat others as we would like to be treated.

It's so important to walk every day with the Lord. The more we read of God's word in the Bible, the more we get his love. The Lord says to meditate on his word, meaning the Bible scriptures. In other words, to think about them a lot.

We need to pray over and over, "Lord, lead me away from temptation." If we resist temptation, it will lessen in time. Also, we won't be so strongly tempted if we ever find ourselves in a tempting environment. But temptation will always be potentially around to entice us, so keep on the alert.

If someone says something hurtful to us, we should resist saying something hurtful back. Instead we should be slow to anger and slow to speak. We should not gossip about people behind their back, and not slander them or run them down. Rather, be a person who builds people up. In addition, do not favour someone because they're wealthy, or look down on someone because they're poor.

Remember, God's love is never ending, it is eternal. He loves us no matter what we do. The Holy Spirit comes to us and comforts us, counsels us and helps us.

So we must live a repentant life and believe in God and love him. We also need to talk to him and sing songs to him and about him.

To repent of a sin also means to stop doing that sin. Ask the Holy Spirit to help us not to sin in whatever area it is.

The voice of God has spoken to me aloud about six times during my life. He did not tell me what to do, but has said such things as, "What are you doing, Adrian?" and "I would not do that If I were you" and "Why are you doing this?"

Something I practice a lot and have done most of my life is to think before I act and think before I speak. This is an important key to spiritual growth. So I repeat it again, "Be slow to speak and slow to anger." Do not function on autopilot. Do not act on impulse and say the first thing that pops into our mind. Think about what we are going to say, and think about what we are going to do. We must try and do the right thing in the eyes of God. It takes practice to do the will of God and it takes practice not to run on autopilot. I cannot stress enough how important this is.

When dealing with other people, it's easy to see their flaws or faults. It's easy to point the finger at someone and say things like "You do this wrong and you shouldn't do that." However, if we stop and think about how we ourselves have our own flaws and faults, then who are we to judge or condemn? Jesus said that the measure we judge others with, will be the same measure that God judges us with. So it's good to remember this and hold our tongue. We are all on our own spiritual journeys, and at different stages of it, so it's good to recognize this and be slow to speak in judgment of others.

If you wish to begin a personal relationship with Jesus today, I recommend you pray this prayer – "Lord Jesus, I invite you into my life. I believe you died for me and that your blood pays for my sins. I now turn from everything I know is wrong. Thank you for the gift of Eternal Life. By faith I receive that gift and I receive you as my Lord and Saviour. Amen".

In praying that way and really meaning it, you will have put your trust in God and Jesus and handed your life over to their care. When you totally put God and Jesus at the top of your priorities, God will make you whole and take away your feeling of emptiness. You will receive the blessing of having good and wonderful things come into your life. You will be provided for and not go without. Peace and wisdom will come to you, and other blessings will soon follow, such as financial miracles.

Stay in God and God will stay in you. God, Jesus and the Holy Spirit are all we need. Make them number one every day and everything else will fall into place and you will have abundance in every way. You will be healed mentally, emotionally and physically. God will take away your old hardened heart and give you a new one that is kind, caring and loving.

Be proud to be on the winning team as a child of God. Be bold in prayer and in life and you will have the courage to overcome fear of people and what they may do to you. God wants us to make the most of our gifts and talents and be successful spiritually and financially. But we must realise that maturity does not come with age, but with acceptance of responsibility.

God's love is unconditional, but his power, works and blessings are conditional on us doing his will, in other words keeping his commandments on love. So be wary of any person who attends church and speaks God's word, but does not do his will. In other words, avoid those who talk the talk but do not walk the talk.

An ounce of obedience is worth a pound of prayer. Glory be to God. Amen

Struggling with addictions?

If you are struggling with addiction, imagine a big cross – the cross Jesus suffered and died on. Place whatever the problem you have at the foot of the cross and then talk to Jesus and ask him to take it from you.

Tell Jesus how you can't handle it or cope with it on your own, and that you need him to take care of it for you. The addiction could be tobacco, alcohol, drugs, or lust – in fact any problem you have.

Then close the door on the problem you have struggled with and suffered from. Leave the door closed and never open it again to indulge, not even one time, and walk the narrow path. But along your way there will be doors you pass that have your addiction or problem written on them. Do not open any one of those doors, because if you open a door even a little bit, the demon we call addiction will leap out and grab you and then consume you.

I also suggest going to AA meetings (Alcoholics Anonymous) for drinking problems and if you have a problem with drugs then there are Narcotics Anonymous (NA) meetings in most cities.

Hallelujah.

Developing supernatural powers

Being able to develop good supernatural powers is much closer to you than you may think. The main key is to have faith and to believe it is possible for you.

One must develop spiritually as well, as they go hand in hand. God has different gifts for different people, so if you find you're not getting one gift, don't worry, God will have some other gift, more suited for you.

Do not lose hope and faith just because you fail to begin with. Keep on being persistent with your development and if you truly desire and believe in supernatural power, then it is within your reach and it will grow and intensify over time.

Being able to predict the future is one of my gifts. It did not happen overnight and it was not until I was 29 that I began prophesying with great accuracy. Even now, it comes and goes in varying intensities, and I'm still not always able to do it. Yet I do not lose hope or faith that I can do it sometimes. I know from experience it can happen for me.

When I'm predicting, messages come through in the form of thoughts. Sometimes they flow and I just speak and out it comes. After I have made a prediction, I usually have a good idea if it is a true one or not. A powerful confidence comes over me when my predictions are real.

A further powerful key is to cast out all doubts and fears, as these will hinder your progress. Ultimately you will fail if you entertain negative thoughts.

Continue to believe, no matter what. Keep trying and you will succeed and discover what it is like to truly believe and to have genuine faith. It will take time, but the more you grow spiritually, the more your supernatural power and ability will grow within you, and the more you will experience all the different aspects of the gift.

Best wishes

Now that my 15-year storm (from the age of 30 to the age of 45) has passed over, I find myself feeling good and doing well mentally and emotionally and no longer depressed. I thank God and the Lord Jesus for this.

In the beginning, following my botched operation, my psychosis and breakdown plagued me severely for about six years. A large part of my mental trauma was a disorder that would allow people's conversations to get stuck in my head, with me going over and over them. I could not find any peace and for those first six years I lived in a lot of fear. However I managed to get free from that symptom, but was still left with a psychotic disorder that affected my mental health at times, but now I seem to be on top of it at last.

God, Jesus and the Holy Spirit have healed me and taken away my desire to drink and to smoke marijuana, which I would do now and then. And I recently gave up smoking tobacco when God removed my desire to smoke. That's fantastic I say.

I have hope and faith that my life will be a lot better from now on. I plan to keep God, Jesus and the Holy Spirit close to me and my main priority in life. I also plan to stay in recovery from alcohol. No harmful substances at all.

I have had much, and I have lost much. Before this nightmare started, I was a doctor of Chinese medicine – an acupuncturist, owning my own home, boats, horse, truck etc, and a life style that went along with all that. Then I lost everything and suffered mentally, emotionally and financially – losing my entire lifestyle as well.

Yet here I am now, with hope and faith that my financial situation will get better and better and I will once again reach financial security. It would love to own my own home once again and to enjoy boating again. It would also be nice to find a lovely Christian spiritual woman and be married to her.

I do hope you have enjoyed reading my book. I trust it has given you hope and faith and perhaps opened your eyes and your mind as well as your heart.

Some people may decide I am a nut, or crazy. This is not a problem for me. I know what I have seen and experienced and I know what was real. I have had so many spiritual experiences with the supernatural that I know within my heart and mind that my stories are all real and true. God gives people different gifts and talents and wants us to use them to their full potential.

God and Jesus have a divine plan for you and for everyone. So nurture a sincere desire to become righteous and Christ-like – to love God wholeheartedly and walk towards your full potential.

As I said earlier, to forgive those who have hurt you, will set you free and allow God and Jesus to forgive you. Leave it to God to deal with those people who have harmed you. God is just. So let go of all resentments and bitterness and hatred.

Do not try and justify any wrong behaviour of the body or the mind, or wrong motives and intentions of the heart. God and Jesus can read our minds – they know the true intentions and motives of our heart.

I know this to be true, and sometimes when I've prayed I have had spiritual experiences of the Holy Spirit, some of which have been extremely powerful. I have also learned that to whisper when I pray is just as powerful as speaking strongly.

If you resist the temptation to sin – to do wrong with your mind or actions, God will see this and honour your efforts and step in and help you.

Again, do not lose hope or faith if God does not answer your prayer right away. Remember, God's timing is always perfect. Sometimes prayers are answered right away and sometimes they are delayed, or the answer is no, because he has other better plans for you.

Faith and believing is powerful. It will change your life. God and Jesus love that you believe in them.

Do not waste your life. Do not reach the end of the one life you have and then have the biggest regret of all – that you failed to reach your maximum potential as the child of God you were born to become. That you did not receive the mercy and forgiveness needed to enter the kingdom of God and receive Eternal Life.

We all have our free will to make these choices, and with these choices, to have the potential to grow spiritually and enter Paradise and enjoy Eternal Life.

If you haven't already done so, repent of your sins and ask for forgiveness of God, and be humble enough to confess to another person the nature of your wrong doing.

Best wishes on your journey to become a new person, a follower of Jesus, set apart from your past and living a Christ-like life.

May you find peace, contentment and joy. May you enter Paradise and be granted Eternal Life.

God bless you, from Adrian.

www.ingramcontent.com/pod-product-compliance
Lightning Source LLC
Chambersburg PA
CBHW052011090426
42741CB00008B/1647